Oriental Designs
in Needlepoint

EVA BRENT

SIMON AND SCHUSTER · NEW YORK

JULIA WEISSMAN, TEXT
GARY TONG, CHARTS
BOB GHIRALDINI, PHOTOGRAPHS
MANUFACTURED IN THE UNITED STATES OF AMERICA

1 2 3 4 5 6 7 8 9 10

LIBRARY OF CONGRESS CATALOGING IN PUBLICATION DATA

BRENT, EVA.
    ORIENTAL DESIGNS IN NEEDLEPOINT.

    BIBLIOGRAPHY: P.
    1. CANVAS EMBROIDERY—PATTERNS.   2. DESIGN,
DECORATIVE—EAST.   I. TITLE.
TT778.C3B74   746.4'4   78-27508
ISBN 0-671-24174-5

ACKNOWLEDGMENTS

It is difficult to know where to start in thanking the friends, customers and others who have given me their precious time and effort for the completion of this book. They are like pieces in a mosaic; without one the whole is incomplete.

I must confess that my deepest gratitude belongs to the little old Chinese man of long ago, who spent his lifetime weaving the magnificent tapestries that inspired the needlepoint in this book.

I thank Gary Tong, who with superb patience drew the graphs, square by little square, preparing each with great accuracy.

My very special thanks to Julia Weissman, for helping me out at a critical time with writing the text. English is my second language and my talents lie with the visual rather than the theoretical.

Thanks to Connie Schrader, my editor. She has given me great freedom in putting this book together, encouraging me subtly and sensitively.

And I thank all the people who have given me their thousands of stitches—Mrs. Sylvana M. DiLaurentiis, Mrs. Dawn Burkhead, Mr. Clint Ide, Mr. James Whitwill, Miss Alicia Tracy, Mrs. J. B. Hoffman, Miss Heda Cohen and Miss Nancy Wagman.

EVA BRENT

CONTENTS

ONE

An Introduction to Oriental Designs

The art of the Orient has intrigued the Western world since the days of Marco Polo. The first European merchants who managed to make their way to the palaces and pagodas of China found much more than tea and spices to take away with them. They found porcelains of a quality and elegance such as they had never seen, as well as a whole array of ornamental robes and hangings made of silk, a fabric still largely unknown in Europe.

It was not just the delicacy of the materials that fascinated the traders; it was the flowing beauty of the Oriental designs—the dreamlike fantasy of the Chinese landscapes and the mysterious charm of the animals portrayed. The superb renderings of birds, flowers, and fishes, whether on ceramics, on scrolls of paper, or on silk, were dazzling to the Western eye.

At the time the Manchu dynasty was established in 1644, the Chinese began to welcome trade with England and the rest of Europe with considerable enthusiasm. Encouraged by the East India Company, England's largest and most powerful importing firm, the Chinese began producing merchandise made especially for European tastes; and sometimes, at the East India Company's request, they copied European designs on their own textiles and ceramics. Chinoiserie, both the European adaptations, which the Chinese obligingly reproduced, and the real thing, became very popular by the end of the seventeenth century. The porcelains and silks of the Orient were avidly sought by discriminating collectors, as they still are today by connoisseurs of antiques.

Japanese art did not become well known until much later, owing to the fact that Japan closed her ports to all foreigners in the mid-sixteenth century after unhappy experiences with Portuguese merchants and with European priests who tried to proselytize and establish missions. Only the Dutch were permitted a trading post at Nagasaki. The bamboo curtain remained firmly closed for more than three centuries, until an American naval officer, Admiral Matthew C. Perry, sailed into Tokyo Bay in July of 1853. After a year of negotiations and pressure, he convinced Japan to reopen trade with the West. Thereafter, Europe and America were introduced to the extraordinary charm of the silk kimono, the allure of Japanese brush painting, and the delights of the *ukiyo-e* prints, as well as pottery and porcelain which, though Chinese in ancestry, were distinctly Japanese in flavor and design.

Whenever we see a beautiful Chinese or Japanese work of art, be it a print, a painting, a gorgeous kimono, an embroidered scene, or a piece of good porcelain, we are struck by its distinctive imagery and fine coloring. The extraordinary quality of the materials and the remarkable workmanship of the Eastern craftsmen and artists are amazing. But there is also a rich symbolism in the birds, flowers, and animals depicted. They frequently represent either desirable virtues or hoped-for good fortune. Even the landscape paintings, so different from traditional Western landscapes, have for the Oriental a spiritual importance beyond the artist's and viewer's mere admiration for beauty.

All the designs I have selected are rich in this symbolism. So in executing them you will not only be recreating works of art; you will be stitching into them deep meaning and a long tradition.

TWO

Needlepoint Embroidery: A Short History

Embroidery is an ancient art form. It probably originated with the invention of bone and thorn needles and developed with the use of plant and animal fibers for thread. The stitches made with this primitive thread could be used to embellish as well as hold together garments and other objects made of animal skins.

When weaving was invented and dyes were developed, embroidery evolved with these two arts. It was used not only to decorate fabric but also to strengthen it and shape it into garments. The desire to fortify cloth probably inspired the earliest precursor of needlepoint—counted thread embroidery in the form of the cross stitch. The decorative stitching on fragments of cloth found in Egyptian tombs dating back to at least 1000 B.C. is almost identical with the basic needlepoint stitches we use today. Both Oriental and European cultures, once they acquired the art of weaving, promptly beautified their textiles with embroidery, either in free-form styles or counted-thread stitchery.

In Roman times needlepoint was considered to be one of the important arts. Pliny the Elder, a Roman scholar and historian who lived during the first century A.D., thought it sufficiently significant to discuss it in some detail in his works. According to Pliny, the Phrygians, who lived in Asia Minor about four hundred years before Christ, were the first people to embroider. (Modern archaeological findings and better research techniques, though, tell quite a different story.) Pliny's version of history also credits the Babylonians as being famous throughout Asia Minor for their embroideries and the varieties of colored yarns they used. The Romans and the Egyptians both favored the counted stitch; they used the cross stitch and the tent stitch on canvas. They called the resulting work *opus pulvinarium*, meaning cushion work.

There is some evidence that the well-developed Anglo-Saxon skill at embroidery and the Roman art of *opus pulvinarium* were joined somewhere around the tenth century A.D. in England. English embroidery became such a sophisticated art during the Middle Ages that it became famous throughout Europe. Known as *opus anglicum* ("English work"), it was highly prized for church vestments. And the royalty and nobility loved to sport their heraldic devices on embroidered horse trappings, bed hangings, and wall coverings.

In Tudor England embroidery was considered a high art and was practiced by both men and women. Embroidery skills were taught to children of the royal house. Henry VIII was said to be an expert, as were Elizabeth I and her cousin, Queen Mary. Queen Elizabeth had a royal court embroiderer by the name of John Parr, and one Edmund Harris served three kings in that same capacity.

Canvas work was often a group activity. Heads of large and rich households often hired full-time professional embroiderers, most of whom were men. These professionals not only possessed great dexterity with the needle but also devised elaborate patterns for others to embroider. Birds, beasts (real and mythical), herbs, and flowers in intricate profusion were popular subjects for embroidery in that time.

You can get some notion of just how important the textile arts were during the Renaissance in Europe from the fact that weaving was officially classed as a major, or "greater," art. European guilds (the artisan unions of the day) were very protective of the rights and privileges of dyers, weavers, woolworkers, and needleworkers. In fact, the popularity of canvas work during the Tudor period would not be surpassed in the Western world until the nineteenth century, when canvas embroidery became simplified by means of painted graph patterns and stamped or stenciled canvases. Many needlework authorities have argued that such commercial shortcuts took all the originality and creativity out of needlepoint and reduced it to a pastime, or "lesser," art.

European and American needlepoint embroiderers of the eighteenth and nineteenth centuries still did some very fine work. They had canvases available in meshes ranging from 18 to 52 threads per inch. In the Colonies, canvas work was done by those who could afford to buy the expensive backing and the necessary amount of wool, but crewel embroidery became more popular because it took much less yarn. However, needlepoint remained a standard form. For instance, Martha Washington made the needlepoint upholstery for ten dining chairs for her Mount Vernon home.

The history of embroidery in the West is fairly well documented, but little is known of the development of the art in the Orient. Historians, however, believe that the Chinese invented the art of embroidery and were practicing it as early as the second millennium B.C., during the Shang dynasty. Careful study of the fragments of wrappings clinging to a bronze vase from that period revealed embroidery with fine silk floss in patterns similar to those of the bronzes and ceramics of the same era. These fragments antedate by a thousand years any other embroidery work known.

There is a gap of several centuries between this work and later pieces of Chinese embroidery. But prose writings and poetry from the literature of the Ch'u kingdom in Hunan and nearby provinces during the Chou and Han periods (1027 B.C. to A.D. 220) make mention of embroidered clothing. And there are some actual examples from the Han dynasty. The very early Chinese embroiderers worked mostly in chain stitch, but later they favored the satin stitch for several decades. For this they used untwisted silk floss, the satiny glossiness of which enhanced the work by providing highlights and an overall sheen.

Fine embroidery soon became an important art in China and Japan, treasured by the aristocracy and the courts of the emperors for use on their ceremonial garments and robes of state. The embroiderers, like their counterparts on the other side of the globe, sometimes originated their own designs but often copied paintings. The most prized, and to this day unsurpassed, embroidery art was created during the Ming dynasty, 1368–1644, a period notable for the exquisite quality of all Chinese arts, especially porcelain. The subtle shadings of Ming embroidered works are as close to painting as is possible with fabric and thread. They are among the greatest of all examples of textile art. During the Ming period, a symbology based on social rank developed. These symbols were embroidered on the clothing that officials wore. The dragon was reserved for the emperor; animals designated nobles and officers; and birds announced the ranks of civil officers.

As in Europe, professional embroidery was often done by men and boys, because they had strong fingers. One characteristic stitch of these Chinese embroiderers was so tiny and was made with such a fine strand of silk that it became known as the "blinding stitch," for it actually strained the eyes of the embroiderer to the point of blindness. This and the satin stitch were to some extent superseded by the counted stitches. Whether the Chinese learned the canvas, or tent, stitches from travelers or imported samples isn't known, but by the eighteenth century they were remarkably adept with the tent stitch as well as with the Florentine flame stitch, which is now known as bargello. However, they still used their superfine silk floss and their ground silk gauze. The Chinese termed these stitches "gauze-stabilizing" stitches.

Around the time that overly bright Berlin yarn was becoming popular in Europe, the Chinese began using aniline dyes to tint their flosses. Their embroideries became, consequently, rather gaudy and lost the elegance that had distinguished them for centuries.

The Chinese techniques for embroidering silk inevitably found their way to Japan. There the kimono, perhaps because of its simple shape, became a vehicle for art. Designs of flowers, birds, and landscapes, when they were not woven into or painted on the fabric, were now embroidered. Japanese textile designs, however, although owing much to Chinese influence, tend to be less elaborate. The Chinese often covered the material completely with embroidery, whereas the Japanese let the fabric show as a supportive background for the embroidery.

Around the turn of this century embroidery lost popularity in both the East and the West, but since World War II a strong do-it-yourself movement has spread throughout the world, and along with it a revival of interest in arts and crafts.

Needlepoint has become especially popular, because it is an ideal lightweight lap art. It is a perfect leisure-time activity. You can do it while watching TV, when traveling, while waiting in the dentist's office, or while resting between sets on the tennis court. It has also established itself as an art form. Even the windows of Tiffany's in New York City have been graced with soft sculpture done in needlepoint. Whether you wear your needlepoint, or carry it, or hang it on a wall, you are sure to be proud of it.

THREE

Materials

CANVAS

Canvas has a long history; in one form or another it was used by the Egyptians, the Romans, and the early Anglo-Saxons. The name comes from *cannabis*, the Latin word for hemp, a plant that for hundreds of years has been converted into fibers used to make rope, sacks, and fabrics.

The first canvas used by the English for their needlework was probably not made of hemp; it was probably linen, which comes from the fiber of the flax plant. Flax was also used by the Egyptians to make linen as fine as silk or as heavy as sailcloth.

Before the Industrial Revolution, the process of turning flax into linen was long and difficult. A 1972 catalogue written by Julia Weissman and Herbert Hemphill for the Museum of American Folk Art reveals: "To turn flax into linen took sixteen months, from planting to finished fabric: sowing, weeding, pulling up the ripened stalks, de-seeding, drying, retting (or rotting) them with a five-day water treatment; cleaning still again, re-drying, and beating several times to remove the woody center; swingled (or scraped) to remove the coarse fibers, then carded with a heavy comb called a hetchel, and recarded several times to refine it into fibers fine enough for spinning into thread or yarn for weaving. Wound into skeins, the thread was bleached in ashes and water for a week, rinsed, washed, dried, and rewound onto weaving bobbins and shuttles. The final fabric itself had to be bleached for weeks in the sun before it was cut, sewed, or embroidered." No wonder linen was cherished and treated with respect! Top-quality linen still takes almost that long, although machines have eased some of the physical labor. Chemical baths have shortened the retting and bleaching time for making inferior linens.

Choosing Needlepoint Canvas. When you go into a needlework shop or the yarn department in a large store to select canvas for the first time, don't expect to see the heavy, closely woven material that is used for beach chairs, awnings, or artists' paintings. Needlepoint canvas is made from stronger fibers and has a more open weave. The openings in the weave are referred to as meshes, and we say that the canvas has a mesh size.

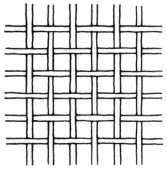
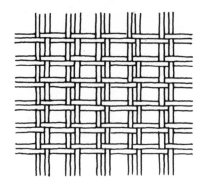

Mono canvas   *Penelope canvas*

There are two kinds of canvas for needlepoint. The first is mono, which is woven with single warp (vertical) threads and single weft (horizontal) threads. In England, mono canvas is known as congress canvas.

The second type, penelope, is a double-thread canvas. Two weft threads instead of one are woven across double warp threads in a simple tabby weave. The advantage of penelope over mono canvas is that the paired threads forming the mesh can be separated when you want to make small stitches. Therefore it allows for a variation in stitch size for fine detailing where your pattern calls for it.

Canvas Sizes. Mesh size can range from the very fine mesh used for petit point embroidery to the very coarse mesh used for making rugs. Practically all canvases are available in both mono weave and penelope weave. Canvas mesh is described by a number. That number, which is called the gauge, represents the number of threads to the inch—not the number of holes. Thus, mono canvas with a gauge number of 10 (#10) has ten threads to the inch. Penelope canvas of the same size has 10 *double* threads to the inch. The penelope canvas will be described as #10/20, meaning you can make as many as twenty stitches or as few as ten stitches to the inch on it.

The most popular gauge, and the one you will probably use for your needlepoint, is mono 14, or penelope 12/24. That is because it is fine enough to allow for small detail work but not so fine as to cause eyestrain. However, you should be aware of the whole range of canvas gauges and of what the various gauges are best suited for.

Petit point refers to canvas with anywhere from 18 to 40 meshes to the inch. It is available in mono or penelope and is suitable for small objects such as eyeglass cases, pincushions, evening bags, wallets, jewelry box tops, and—for the ambitious—needle "paintings."

Gros point in a mono canvas can run from 10 to 18 threads per inch. In penelope it may have from 8 to 12 threads per inch.

Quick point canvas is quite coarse, with as few as 3 to 7 heavy threads to the inch. Quick point is available in mono or penelope and is most often used for rugs. Seven-thread, or #7, canvas is the finest of the quick point canvases and is used for small, lightweight rugs that have a certain amount of detail. The larger meshes are fine for splashier patterns.

Canvas Widths. Canvas usually comes in widths of from 18 to 54 inches. Because petit point canvases are most often used for small projects, they are usually 36 inches wide. Gros point canvases are frequently much wider.

Quick point, or rug, canvas is usually from 36 to 54 inches wide.

Buying Canvas. Canvas comes in three standard colors: white, yellow, and ecru. Since the threads of the canvas will be completely covered by the needlepoint yarn, it doesn't matter which of these colors you use.

The finish of the canvas, or the sizing, a special starchlike substance that gives it its stiff feeling, is the same on both sides, so there is no wrong or right side. Therefore, a design may be drawn, painted, or printed on either side. Like all woven fabrics, canvas has selvedges, or tightly woven edges, all around to keep it from raveling.

Needlepoint canvas can be made of cotton, linen, or synthetic fibers. Cotton and linen canvases are more expensive than synthetic ones, but they are worth the additional investment. Because of the sizing, all canvas is stiff when you buy it, but cotton and linen become supple and tractable as you work on them. Canvas made of synthetic fiber, however, goes limp and loses body and shape.

Even if you choose the most expensive canvas, examine it carefully before you buy it. Good canvas should have smooth threads without lumps or knots, and it should have square, evenly spaced meshes. If it has been properly sized, it will be a bit stiff and have a slightly glossy, or polished, look.

How Much Canvas to Buy. Before you start a needlepoint design, decide what you are going to use it for. Will it be a pillow, a piano bench cover, upholstery for a dining chair, a cover for a waste basket, a tote bag? Will it be appliquéd onto a vest or jacket? Will you frame it like a painting?

If you want to make a pillow, for instance, decide on the size and shape. (It is quite possible, you know, to make needlepoint pillows that are not round or rectangular.) If you plan to cover an object, you must measure the object. Be sure to measure not only its maximum length but also its widest and narrowest dimensions.

Next make a paper pattern exactly the size of the object or surface you wish to cover. Then add four inches to the *maximum* width and the *maximum* length, or two inches all around. This will assure that you have enough canvas to attach or finish off the completed work. It will also allow for any shrinkage after blocking, and it will prevent any bare canvas from showing on the edges of the finished project.

Of course, a small item will not require that much margin. Use your judgment, but a half inch too much is always better than a half inch too little.

Preparing the Canvas for Work. If your canvas is not exactly the desired size, you may have to cut it down. In doing so, you will cut off one or more of the selvedges on the edge of the canvas. Be sure to finish off any raw or cut edges so that they won't ravel while you work. The simplest way of finishing is to bind the cut edges with tape. You can use masking tape or any flexible plastic or fabric tape that sticks well.

Bind the raw edges of any small pieces you cut off, and save these scraps. They will come in handy for practice and for patching. Accidents happen to the best of us, you know! Furthermore, sometimes these salvaged pieces are big enough to be used for small projects. Put these extra pieces away where you can find them again.

The Design on the Canvas. For many people needlepoint is a very personal art medium; the needles are the brushes, and the wools are the paints. Such people like to create their own designs and paint them on the canvas themselves. I know of one needlepoint artist who neither draws nor paints on the canvas. She simply designs the work in her head, creating it as she stitches.

Other people may find that designing a canvas is a little frightening until they have gained a bit of practice and confidence. These people may prefer the painted or printed canvas, which will guide them into pleasing designs and attractive color combinations.

There is, incidentally, no rule that says a design must be embroidered exactly as printed. A printed design can be adapted to look quite different from the printed original by changing the color scheme, by adding new details, or by reversing the direction of a motif. Unfortunately, preprinted or painted canvases are often rather expensive, so the embroiderer may hesitate to modify them. But don't stifle your creative urges.

I hope that this book will convince you that even if you can't design your own needlepoint and can't afford to buy a prepainted or preprinted canvas, you can still do beautiful needlepoint by using the graph method of following a pattern stitch by stitch or by transferring a design to your own canvas.

Using a Frame. Many professionals advise using a rectangular frame when doing needlepoint. They feel it keeps the canvas on grain better and makes for even stitching. Frames usually consist of two cross bars (top and bottom) with strong canvas strips between them. These bars fit into side bars in such a way that they can be adjusted up or down. The needlepoint canvas is sewn to the top and bottom bars and laced to the side bars. Some frames can be braced so they are at an angle between your lap and a table edge. Others come on stands and can be tipped up or down.

I personally do not favor frames except, possibly, for large pieces that might be awkward to maneuver. Frames can be uncomfortable as well as a nuisance to work on, especially when you do the continental stitch, which requires constant turning of the canvas. They are cumbersome to travel with, and you certainly can't use them in a car or on a bus or plane trip. The prime advantage of a frame is that it eliminates the need for blocking. But if you plan to have your work mounted by a professional, the blocking is always included anyway, so not much is gained.

Needlepoint is an ideal lap art, and doing it is very personal; your way of stitching and your handling of the canvas as you work are part of what makes it your own. Your technique is in a sense your fingerprint; perhaps that is what makes needlepoint such a special, personal gift.

Having said that, let me not stop you. If you like perfection and don't mind the discomfort of using a frame, by all means use one.

Although some experts feel you should never use a round embroidery frame for needlepoint—they insist it pulls the canvas and stretches it out of shape—there are others who endorse a round frame, saying that it is acceptable if it makes the work easier for you. You should, however, be careful when using an embroidery hoop. It can cause some unevenness in the canvas shape.

NEEDLES

Embroidery needles have a very long history. The first ones were undoubtedly made of fishbones or thorns (in parts of Mexico, cactus thorns are still used for needles). Bronze needles made by the Etruscans and found in Rome date back as far as 700 B.C. The Chinese were making steel needles several centuries before the birth of Christ. The Moors introduced them to Spain via the Near East during the sixteenth century. When such needles appeared in London, they were called Spanish needles. They were not exactly new to the English, because metal needles had been made in the Redditch area of Worcestershire since before Roman times.

When you go to buy needles for needlepoint, ask for *tapestry* needles. They differ from regular embroidery needles in that their points are rounded and blunt rather than sharp. The point is rounded so that it will pass smoothly through the mesh openings without catching on the canvas threads, or will separate the threads in penelope canvas without splitting the warp or weft. The eye of a tapestry needle is long and open so that it will accommodate several strands of yarn at a time.

Tapestry needles come in different sizes. The larger the number, the smaller the canvas gauge they are suited for and the fewer strands of yarn they will hold. The chart on page 20 will be helpful when it comes to selecting the proper needle.

A Word of Advice. Individual tapestry needles, unlike sewing machine needles, do not have the size marked on them. It is prudent, therefore, to keep one or two needles in the original package and to make sure the size label remains firmly attached. If you get confused about the size needle you are using, you can check it against the ones left in the package.

CANVAS GAUGE (Mono)	NEEDLE SIZE
24 through 32	24
16 through 18	22 or 24
10 through 14	18 or 20

(Penelope)	
21 through 32	24
16 through 18	22 or 24
10 through 14	18 or 20
7 or 8	14
3 through 5	13

How to Thread Needlepoint Needles. This is more easily demonstrated than described, but basically, what you do is this: Loop a couple of inches of yarn over the eye end of the needle, pull it tight, and hold needle and looped thread tightly between your thumb and forefinger so that you can just barely see the thread. Slide the needle out of the loop, lay the eye of the needle over the top of the loop, and push the wool through. It takes a little practice, but once you get the hang of it, you'll even thread your sewing needles this way. If the technique escapes you, however, don't be shy about using a needle threader.

YARN

Many people are lured into doing needlepoint simply because the yarns are so lusciously beautiful. There is something about the lively springiness of softly gleaming wool, the satiny shine of good embroidery cotton, and the fabulous shades they come in that almost begs you to do something with them.

By far the favorite embroidery yarn for needlepoint is wool. It is the most durable, and almost any kind of wool yarn, except soft knitting wool, can be used. Still, there are people who use cotton embroidery thread exclusively, although it tends to twist more easily and is more subject to fading.

Silk is sometimes used to highlight special details, but it is expensive and harder to work with than wool, so you should avoid it if you are a beginner.

The same is true for metallic threads. They are very costly, and it takes considerable skill to work with them. Rayon embroidery thread, though temptingly lustrous and brilliant, should be avoided because it tends to twist constantly and frays excessively.

So let's talk about wools. The two most commonly used needlework wool yarns are Persian and crewel.

Persian Yarn. The best known of the Persian wools is probably the Paternayan. It is a long-fibered, three-ply yarn with a lovely, light-catching sheen. (Ply indicates the number of strands in a thread.) It is available in a wide spectrum of colors (343 at last count) in group gradations of from three to seven shades per color. The name Persian comes from the fact that the Paternayan brothers, who came to the United States in 1923, were originally in the business of importing and dyeing Persian wool yarns to repair Aubusson and Persian carpets. Exactly when they added wools for embroidery isn't known.

I prefer Persian wool. It is mothproofed (as are most wools these days); it wears well because of the long fibers; and the strands are easily separated, which means you can use one, two, or three strands at a time, or add more strands to make a thicker ply if necessary. A further advantage of Persian is that you can develop interesting color schemes or visual textures with it by mixing strands of different shades or even different colors.

If Paternayan wool is not available where you are, DMC, an old and respected manufacturer of embroidery threads, makes a three-strand Persian yarn for needle-point use in some 224 colors.

Crewel Yarn. Crewel embroidery traditionally features flowers and leaves and is done in assorted freehand stitches. Crewel embroidery is distinguished from canvas work by the fact that it is not a counted-stitch embroidery. Back in 1882 Sophia Frances Anne Caulfield defined crewel in her *Dictionary of Needlework* as: "Worsted yarn, loosely twisted. In early times known as *caddis, caddas,* or *crule.* Derived from Anglo-Saxon *cleow,* afterwards changed to *clew* (a ball of thread); and subsequently called *cruell* or *krewell,* old German *kluel.*"

Modern crewel is a two-ply yarn primarily used for embroidery, but because it is a long-fibered wool that doesn't fray easily, it is also suitable for needlepoint. The plies separate quite easily, so you can combine it, if you like, with Persian wool. For instance, if you can't find that special color or blend you want in the wide variety available in Paternayan and DMC, you might be able to devise it with crewel. Used as is, though, crewel will not cover quite as well as the Persian yarns, so you may have to add an extra strand. It will depend on your mesh gauge.

Tapestry Yarns. The tapestry yarn that weavers use may also be used in needle-point. It is a strong, four-ply wool, but because of the tight twist, the plies aren't easily separated, so it is best used as it is. Therefore, I recommend it only when you are working with 12- to 14-gauge canvas. Paternayan tapestry wools come in about 250 colors, and DMC makes about 430 colors.

Cotton Embroidery Thread. If you prefer to embroider with cotton rather than wool, use a sufficient number of strands so that the thickness approximates that of the Persian yarn you would use for the same mesh canvas. The same rule applies to crewel yarns.

Far and away the most popular cotton embroidery thread is DMC, which has six strands and comes packaged in small hanks. The DMC company, which has been producing thread for over 230 years, is located in France. Its yarns are exported all over the world. Because of its brilliancy of color and its glossiness, DMC embroidery thread is a fairly good substitute for silk. It is considerably less costly and far easier to handle. The strands are easy to separate, so it can be made thicker or thinner, and it can be mixed. Some people use it in combination with silk, but I don't recommend doing so.

If you live in a large city, or one with a really good art needlework shop, you can sometimes find interesting cotton embroidery threads from other companies. For instance, the Coulter Studios, a fascinating shop in New York City that caters to fiber artists and carries all kinds of yarns, has a pretty cotton embroidery thread called Parisian, which is fine for needlepoint. It is six-ply, but the plies are wound in such a way that they cannot be separated, so like tapestry yarn it must be used as is.

Calculating Your Yarn Needs. The amount of yarn you need for a particular design or pattern will depend on the size of the piece you want to make and on how you embroider; that is, whether your stitching tends to be loose or tight. The gauge of the canvas is also a factor, as is the kind of stitch. For example, the basketweave stitch requires almost twice as much yarn as the continental stitch. Then, too, you have to take into account that accidents do happen, and there will therefore be some ripping out.

After you've selected the gauge canvas you are going to use and decided on the ply yarn it takes, work a one-inch square of canvas in the stitch or stitches the design will be done in. Keep note of how much yarn this takes. If you are working from a graph, make an approximation of the number of square inches there will be in each color. If, however, you have transferred your design directly onto the canvas, do the following: Get a sheet of clear acetate paper the size of your canvas and some indelible ink at an art supply store. Using a ruler and the indelible ink, draw one-inch squares on the acetate. Attach the acetate over your painted canvas with masking tape. Now you can easily estimate the inches to be covered by each color, and from that you can figure out how much yarn of each color you will need. (Keep that acetate sheet. You'll be using it again and again for future projects. It will save you time, money, and yarn!)

Obviously, it is impossible to determine the exact amount of each color you will need. But there is a sort of rule of thumb you can use. First of all, you should always have at least five percent more yarn than you actually need. So if you think you need 20 skeins, buy 21 skeins—just to be safe. This is based on the assumption that, generally speaking, one strand of yarn will cover one square inch of canvas. Adding five percent to that estimate will allow for weaving in the beginnings and ends of strands, carry-overs, and some ripping out and redoing.

Once you know how many strands you will need, assuming a strand is 18 inches long, you can calculate how many yards you will need (two strands make one yard), and your yarn shop will help you from there.

Persian yarns are generally sold by the pound and tapestry yarns in 40-yard skeins. The yarn shop will convert the Persian yardage you need into pounds (or vice versa). Naturally, if you intend to split the Persian yarn into one or two strands, you won't need as much; whereas if you plan to increase the ply, you will need more.

But always buy some extra! Yarns are dyed in batches, or lots. If you run out, it isn't always possible to get an exact match. Although the dye formulas may never change, they don't always come out exactly the same shade on the next batch of wool. Each day's dye batch may, for various reasons such as weather and slight differences in the yarn, absorb the dye just a little differently than the previous day's dye batch. Therefore, each new batch of yarn is given a new lot number. Slight differences in tones tend to be magnified on the finished work. That's why it is important to buy your yarn by the lot number as well as by color, and why embroiderers, weavers, and knitters are urged to get a little more yarn than actually seems necessary when they are buying for a project. My advice is to buy generously—especially for backgrounds. It is better to have some yarn left over than to run short!

But suppose you *do* run out of yarn. Is everything lost? Not really, if you are working with two- or three-ply yarn. When you get down to your last ten strands of yarn, you can usually tell pretty well whether or not you are going to have enough to finish the job. If you think you'll run short, stop right where you are and go and buy more yarn. Take the yarn you have with you. If you can't get the same lot number, match the color as closely as you can.

When you get home, cut the new yarn into the same length strands as the old. Separate all the plies of the old lot and the new lot into single-ply strands. Then mix the old batch with the new batch into two- or three-ply strands. You may have two new strands to one of the original lot. The difference, which is apt to be slight, will blend sufficiently so that it won't be too noticeable. Probably no one—except you, if you look very closely—will be able to detect any difference.

Avoid storing your wool and canvas in airtight plastic bags. Wool, which is a natural fiber, needs to "breathe"; otherwise it gets dry and mats.

When you buy wool in hanks, skeins, or balls, cut it into 18-inch lengths. Longer lengths twist, knot, and fray after a while, and that can get very irritating. There is a marvelous gadget called a Point Pack, which is made of two pieces of lucite hinged together like a notebook. It has rounded slots at the top, and when you set it up like a screen, you can drape your strands of wool through these slots.

OTHER NECESSITIES

Before we get down to the important matter of learning the stitches that will be used to work the designs in this book, let's assemble the other basic materials you should have on hand before starting to work. These tools will help you to create smooth, neat-looking work.

You will need a tote bag or a smoothly lined basket large enough to hold the canvas without too much crushing and enough of the wool for several hours' work. The tote bag should also include a ditty box, or what our grandmothers called an *etui*, to hold small tools and other items.

Thimbles. I know there are people who absolutely abhor working with a thimble; perhaps you are one. If you want to enjoy doing needlepoint, make some effort to overcome your disaffection for this most helpful tool. Pushing a needle with your bare finger can get quite painful and can leave your finger looking very punished. If you find a metal thimble objectionable, then start with one of those rubber thimbles that cashiers use to count paper money. You can find them in office supply stores and stationery shops. Once you get used to the rubber protector, you can probably make an easy transition to a metal thimble. A friend told me that she always hated thimbles until she found a charming antique silver one that looked so pretty she actually enjoyed wearing it.

Get two or three thimbles so that if one is misplaced, you won't waste hours looking for it. A thimble should fit closely enough so that it doesn't slip off, but not so tightly that it is uncomfortable. If you cherish long nails, use a thimble with a hole in the top and push the needle with the side of the thimble. Plastic or metal thimbles are both fine, but avoid bejeweled thimbles; they snag the wool and canvas.

Scissors. Buy the best-quality small, sharp, finely pointed embroidery scissors, and use them for cutting wool *only*. If you use them to cut canvas or paper, you will ruin them.

Shears. Regular dressmaker shears will do. Use them for cutting the canvas.

A Sand or Emery Bag. This is for polishing your needles if they tarnish or get rough. You can get these in a variety store or a notions department. All you do is push the needle in and out a few times, and *voilà!* it looks like new. These bags are inexpensive and handy items.

Extra Needles. Always! Needles get lost, are misplaced, mysteriously disappear. Keep some extra needles in the package they come in, or in clear plastic pill bottles, or in a small box. Do not put a variety of sizes in a container. Separate them and be sure to indicate the needle size on the container. This takes a few extra minutes, but it will save you time in the long run.

Tweezers. The sharp pointed kind are best. They are a must when you remove stitches (nobody is perfect) and have to pick off the fuzz that is left in the canvas meshes.

Ruler or Yardstick. For measuring and for drawing lines.

Measuring Tape. Use the non-stretch kind, for measuring the item you intend to cover and for general measuring.

Pencil. Use a No. 2 or softer.

Waterproof India Ink.

Brushes. Have an assortment of fine artists' brushes, but not necessarily the expensive sable kind.

Waterproof Dry Marker Pens. Have an assortment in different colors. Be sure to test every marker on a piece of scrap canvas. Let it dry well and then wet it to make sure the color doesn't run.

Dressmaker's Carbon. For tracing patterns onto canvas.

Graph Paper. Have both opaque and transparent for copying designs.

Acetate Film. For tracing designs. This can usually be found in art supply stores.

Acrylic Paints. For painting designs on canvas. Acrylic paints are water-soluble and so can be easily thinned with a little water. But they are waterproof when dry. Experiment with them first on paper and on canvas scraps to become familiar with how they mix and how fast they dry. Caution: Your brush must be kept in water at all times. Don't allow the paint to dry on it, or it will be ruined. I've found that acrylic paints are easier to use and have less of a lingering odor than oil paints, but you can use oil paints if you prefer them.

Magnifying Glass. This is helpful for seeing stitches when you are working from a graph.

FOUR

Basic Stitches and Techniques

There are at least twenty popular needlepoint or canvas embroidery stitches, and many of these stitches have several variations, but they all start with the same skeleton: a half cross stitch which crosses the intersection of one vertical thread and one horizontal thread at the angle where they intersect.

It's often fun to use several different stitches when you want to make a piece with a mixed textural quality. But since the designs I have developed for this book are adapted from the antique arts of the Orient, it seems appropriate to do them in the oldest known canvas stitch. This stitch has been used by the Chinese and Japanese as well as by needleworkers in the Western world for over 1,000 years. It is the tent stitch, which is really composed of two stitches, the continental stitch and the basketweave (or diagonal tent) stitch. These two stitches are basic and can be used for any design on any size canvas, from the finest petit point to the coarsest mesh rug canvas. The Chinese used it on silk gauze, with silk floss as embroidery yarn!

Because canvas sewn with the tent stitch resembled tapestry weaving, early needlepoint was often referred to as needlework tapestry. Early artists also discovered that the tent stitch made canvas embroidery suitable for cushions and upholstery. The underside of the canvas is covered with more thread or yarn than the upper, and this contributes considerably to the durability of the finished work.

If this is your first effort at needlepoint, let me suggest that you do not try to follow instructions with your mind's eye only. Instead, take a fairly large piece of scrap canvas and a threaded needle and practice the stitch. If you refer to the diagrams as well as to the text while you work, you will accomplish two things. You will learn the stitches, and you will learn how to pull the yarn so that your stitch is neither too loose nor too tight. It really doesn't take much practice before you are able to turn out an even, beautiful piece of embroidery.

Always remember, *all* needlepoint stitches go from one mesh to the other by diagonally crossing the mesh intersections from *left* to *right*. This applies whether you are working across the canvas horizontally, or down it vertically, or at an angle.

THE CONTINENTAL STITCH

There are two rules about this stitch. First, it should be used for outlining and for those very small places in the design where the basketweave just won't work. The continental stitch should be avoided for filling in backgrounds because it tends to pull the canvas "off grain" to such an extent that it is almost impossible to block it into shape.

The second rule is that you *always* start at the *right* and go left, and when the row is finished, you turn the canvas completely upside down, so that once again you are going from right to left. You will know if you've made a mistake and done two rows in the same direction. Doing so produces an unattractive ridge, and no amount of pulling of the canvas or blocking will remove the ridge. You just have to take out the row and do it correctly; that's all there is to it.

Anchoring starting strand

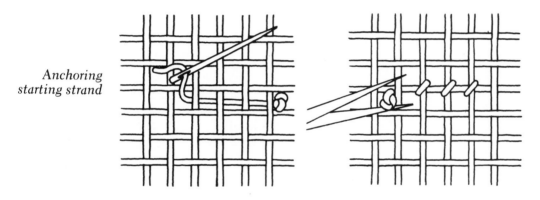

To begin the continental stitch, thread your needle and tie a knot at the end of the yarn. At about an inch to the *left* of the mesh hole that will be the beginning of the first stitch, and on the same line as the mesh hole, put the needle through the canvas from the front and take it over to the mesh where the first stitch will begin. (See diagram.) Bring the needle up from the back through to the front of the canvas. As you continue to stitch, that tail will be anchored to the back of the canvas. When you reach the knot on the front work surface (you will be embroidering toward it), take your embroidery scissors and snip it off *from the back*. With your pointed tweezers, pick the knot off. The end of the strand is anchored securely by being stitched under and over the horizontal or vertical stitches on the back of the canvas. When you start with a new strand of yarn, weave about an inch of the end of the new piece into the back of the design on the underside of the canvas. That will anchor it, and the joining of the new and old yarn will be invisible.

To Do the Continental Stitch Horizontally (Across). Bring your wool up from the back of the canvas to the front and insert the needle one mesh to the right just

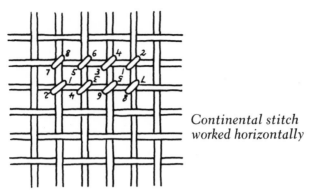

*Continental stitch
worked horizontally*

above the first mesh, crossing the intersection diagonally. Insert the needle but do not pull the wool through. Now insert the point of the needle one mesh below and two meshes to the left and pull the yarn through. (See diagram.) Now cross the mesh intersection one mesh to the right just above, insert the needle, and bring it through one mesh below and two to the left. Continue in this manner. When you get to the end of the row, don't insert your needle two meshes to the left. Instead, insert it one mesh below the last stitch, pull the wool through, and turn the canvas completely around and *upside down.* You can now repeat the stitch back across the canvas, from right to left.

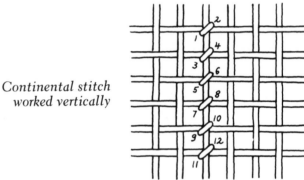

*Continental stitch
worked vertically*

   To Do the Continental Stitch Vertically (Downward). Bring the needle up from the back and cross the intersection one mesh above and to the right. Insert the needle and bring it two meshes down to the left. Pull the needle and yarn through, crossing the intersection at a diagonal one mesh above to the right. Repeat. (See diagram.) If you have to do another row, turn your canvas upside down so that you will be going counter to the first row.

THE BASKETWEAVE STITCH (DIAGONAL TENT STITCH)

While the continental stitch is what might be called the "drawing" stitch of needle-point, because it is used for outlining, the basketweave stitch is the "painting" stitch.

With this stitch you fill in the background of the design. In surface appearance, the basketweave stitch looks like the continental, which is why they go together. But on the back side of the canvas, it looks like tabby weaving.

As with the continental stitch, make sure that you do not work two successive rows in the same direction. However, if you remember the following little rule, chances of such an error are minimized. In doing the basketweave stitch, always make two stitches next to each other horizontally; and then two stitches, one under the other, vertically.

Since the basketweave is worked on the diagonal from top to bottom and bottom to top, there is no need to keep turning the canvas around. The basketweave stitch doesn't pull the canvas off grain or out of shape, or at least, if done properly, not so much that it can't be blocked back into proper alignment and on the square.

To prevent further distortion or pulling of the canvas, particularly to prevent it from being pushed into an awkward, unblockable bulge in the middle, start working at the center of the design, or as near the center as possible, and then work outward in all directions.

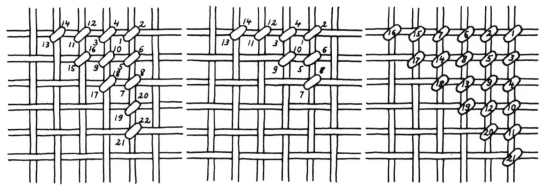

Basketweave stitch

To begin the basketweave stitch, make the first two stitches as if you were doing the continental stitch horizontally. (See stitches marked 1, 2, 3, and 4.) But for the third stitch, don't go left horizontally; instead, move two meshes down, bring the needle up (5), and cross the intersection one mesh above and one to the right (6). Push the needle through, bring it up one mesh to the left and two meshes down (7), and cross the intersection one mesh above and to the right (8). Push the needle through, bring it out two meshes left (9), and cross the intersection one mesh above and to the right (10). Push the needle in, bring it out two meshes left (11), and cross the intersection right and above (12). Put the needle in, bring it out left two meshes and down one mesh (13), and cross the intersection right and above and put it in (14).

If you look at your work and at the diagram at this point, you will see that you are working in a triangular pattern. Keep working this way until you reach the outlining continental stitches of the section you are working on; then, studying the diagram, work your way back down to the right and up left.

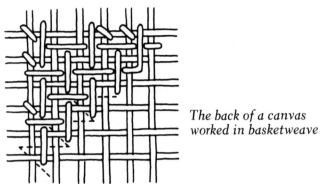

The back of a canvas worked in basketweave

After you have done a section, turn your canvas over to the wrong side, and you will see why this is called the basketweave stitch.

The basketweave is a soothing, very satisfying embroidery stitch. As you work your yarn into the canvas, the design seems to flow out from your fingers like paint on paper.

As in knitting, when you put your work down and take it up later, it isn't always easy to remember in which direction you were going. So the thing to do is to leave the needle (with the yarn in it) tucked in the canvas in the direction in which you were going. Do this even if you are at the end of the yarn. Or else leave a little tail of yarn hanging. This is especially important if you are working with two or three colors in different parts of the canvas. You can weave those ends in when you pick up the work again.

Check your stitches to make sure they are all slanting in the same direction. Any you see that are slanting the wrong way will have to be ripped out and corrected. Don't be discouraged by this. It happens to everyone.

One reason for practicing on a scrap before you begin the actual project is so that, among other things, you will see if your wool is covering the canvas; that is, if you are using a sufficient number of strands. After you have done a reasonable amount of work on the actual project, check from time to time to see that you have not missed any stitches. If you have, fill them in.

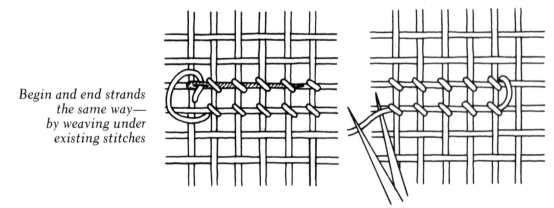

Begin and end strands the same way— by weaving under existing stitches

When you begin a strand or end one, weave it under and over the back stitches on the horizontal or diagonal. Try not to finish or begin strands too close to one

another or over one another. This can create a bump on the front side.

When you trim the end of a finished strand, cut it as close as possible to prevent bits of lint from getting caught in the next stitches. This tends to dull surface colors.

IF YOUR WORK IS TIGHT

If you are finding it hard to pull your needle through or to weave in the end of the yarn strand, then you are working too tightly. That can take the pleasure out of the whole thing as well as affect the final appearance of the needlepoint. Take a little time right now and learn how to ease your stitching; the work will go more easily, and the results will please you.

Take a piece of canvas; one of the scrap pieces you have will do perfectly. Put the threaded needle through one of the meshes, just as if you were starting a stitch. But *don't pull*. Once the needle is through, let the yarn go through the canvas and then let it stop, almost of its own accord. Be careful not to tug or yank the yarn. Then put the needle through again, and once more, when it is all the way through, just let the yarn follow along through the canvas. Continue doing this for some time. The stitches will be bumpy, even loose, but after a while you will automatically get the right tension and will learn, just by feel, to pull just enough to keep the stitches even but not so much as to make them unworkably tight.

Sometimes, if you have trouble with tight stitching, it may help to use a needle the next size smaller than the needle recommended for the mesh canvas you are using.

As a last resort, use a doubled single strand of yarn. However, this works only on #12 or #14 canvas.

The most effective cure is to go back to square one and retrain yourself. It doesn't take long, and the results are worth it!

USEFUL HINTS

When you are ready to start, organize your yarn in color groups and cut it into strands about 18 inches long. It saves a bit of time, too, to thread several needles at once.

If you have to rip out just a few stitches, take them out stitch by stitch. Unthread your needle, turn the canvas over and pull the thread from the back, then turn it over and pull it from the front, using the head, or eye, end of the needle as a tool. It sounds tedious, but it is much the easiest method.

If a lot of stitches have to come out, either snip them out or use the system just described, but *don't reuse the yarn*. It will be too frayed and weakened. Also, be sure to clean away any bits of lints or fuzz left in the canvas meshes with your fine tweezers.

Try to work each strand of wool to its end, even if it means skipping over the canvas an inch or two. Small lengths of wool aren't good for much except filling in a missing stitch or two. If the space you are skipping over has been worked in another color, just weave through those stitches. If you have to skip quite a long space, cut the yarn, weave the end under several stitches, and save whatever is left.

Yarn tends to get twisted as you embroider. Some of this can be prevented by giving the needle a half turn before each stitch. But it may become necessary to hold the canvas up and let the needle and thread dangle so that the yarn will untwist itself.

Always work your design in first and check for any mistakes or color changes you might want to make. Then work in the background.

When accidents happen (and they do), don't panic. Say you are cutting out some stitches and you cut a thread or two of canvas. Just rip out a few stitches around this doleful misstep; then pull some extra threads of canvas from one of your scraps, lay them carefully over the cut canvas, and daub them with a *tiny* bit of Elmer's white glue or colorless nail polish. Let it dry overnight, then rework the spot.

If something really terrible happens to cause a big rip or tear, or if a pet chews what you've done and leaves a hole, be calm. Take out enough stitches from all around the hole to make a rectangle with about a half-inch margin of canvas. Then get a scrap of canvas and cut it into a square or rectangle that will fit over the hole. Baste it onto the canvas so that warp and weft threads match exactly. (Fastidious people sometimes weave the patch in, but it isn't necessary.) Now just embroider the tragedy out of sight. When the work is done and blocked, it will be out of mind as well.

Always wash your hands without fail before you begin to work. And look before you put your work down, to make sure you aren't putting it on a magazine or a newspaper. Newsprint is one step below carbon paper in its ability to smudge.

FIVE

Graphs and Canvas Design

WORKING WITH GRAPHS

Doing needlepoint by following a design printed on a graph is not a new idea. It dates back, in fact, to the late eighteenth century. To make stitch counting easier, canvas manufacturers began producing canvas in which every tenth warp thread was a dark color. Around 1804, a print seller in Berlin saw the connection between that kind of canvas and graph paper and developed a method of printing designs on graph paper, with a symbol and color code printed down the side. Shortly thereafter, these graph-printed patterns were not only color-coded, they were hand-colored. One of the companies that made them, L. Wittich of Berlin, went so far as to hire trained artists to copy famous paintings and translate them into needlepoint patterns by reducing them to squares on "point" paper. These graph-printed patterns were extremely popular throughout Europe and the United States until the last quarter of the nineteenth century. Because of them, "canvas work," as needlepoint was then called, also became known as Berlin work.

For me, one of the exciting things about needlework is that although new ideas and new patterns are constantly coming forth, every needleworker, whether knowingly or unknowingly, is working within a long, rich tradition in every piece of canvas.

It's rare these days to find needlepoint canvas woven with a dark thread at every tenth warp and weft as it was 175 years ago. Therefore, you must mark your own canvas to correspond to the graph. This is not at all difficult.

Graph paper is printed in tiny squares, with every tenth horizontal line and every tenth vertical line printed heavier than the others. Each square formed by these heavier lines contains 100 small squares. Each square represents one stitch.

After you have cut your canvas to size, bind the edges with tape. Fold the canvas in half vertically and then again in half horizontally, so that it is divided into four rectangles. Mark the point where thse two folds intersect with a cross. You can baste the mark in or draw it lightly with a pencil. That cross is the center of your canvas. Look at the graphs of the designs in the book, and indicate an X in the center of each design that you use. To establish the center of the graph, draw two diagonal lines from upper to lower corners with a pencil. The point where they cross is the center. The X has not been indicated, but you can easily count the charted stitches and divide by two.

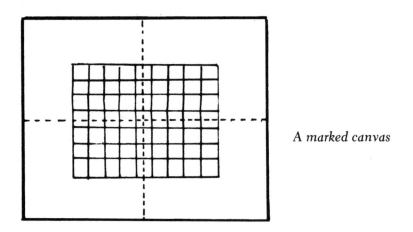

A marked canvas

Using a pencil, draw a light line along the horizontal fold and another light line along the vertical fold. Mark the top of your canvas. (It will be taped, so just write "Top" on the tape.)

Now look at the graph again. Count the small squares from the center X to the top of the graph. Count off the same number of meshes in your canvas from the center, and draw a horizontal line across the canvas. Do the same at the bottom and on both sides. The resulting rectangle on your canvas will be the outline for the design.

Next, draw light lines on the canvas to correspond to the heavy lines on the graph; that is, every ten meshes across and every ten meshes vertically.

If you want to simplify matters for yourself, take this book to a copy printer and have the design you want to make photocopied in a larger size. A photocopy is not at all expensive, and a larger size is much easier to work with. Don't forget to have the color code included! You can, if you feel like it, emulate that German print seller and color the enlarged design according to the color code. Or you can transfer the pattern to the canvas itself and paint it in. The following section will tell you how. (Quantities of yarn needed for each design are not given. It is impossible to determine the absolute amount, considering the human factor, variations in stitch tension, and the more or less economic handling of yarn. On page 43 instruction is given for determining quantities.)

PAINTING AND DESIGNING YOUR OWN CANVAS

For some needlepoint embroiderers, working by following a graph presents no problems. Others, however, particularly beginners, find it much easier to work with a canvas on which the design has been sketched and the color scheme has been painted in. This you can do yourself.

You don't have to be a trained artist to put a design on canvas. A little courage, a venturesome spirit, and the proper materials will turn the trick. As a matter of fact, with a small amount of ingenuity you can even create your own original designs, and I feel certain you will enjoy doing so if you like doing needlepoint.

Suppose you want to transfer a design right onto the canvas. First of all, any design will be easier to follow if you have it enlarged by a photocopier. Have it enlarged to the size the finished design will be. Do not allow the design to reach the edge of the canvas. Remember, you'll need about two inches on every side for finishing.

Mark the center of the design clearly. Then take a piece of tracing paper or clear acetate and trace the enlargement. (Acetate is preferable, because unless you are using an indelible pen or marker, once you no longer need the tracing, you can simply wipe it off with a damp cloth and use the acetate again and again. Also, acetate is tougher than tracing paper, so it does not tear or wrinkle as easily.) Compare the tracing with the enlargement to make certain you have included all the details. Then go over the tracing with a very black pencil or marker. Mark the center, and using a straightedge, carefully draw lines across the top, bottom, and sides to be sure the design is squared off properly.

Next, spread a piece of heavy white paper or some white sheeting a little larger than your canvas on a table or flat surface large enough to accommodate it; a large table should be adequate for most projects. Place your tracing on this surface, and place the canvas on top of the tracing. Match up the center of the design with the center of the canvas. Secure the canvas at the top with masking tape so it won't slide around. You should be able to see the tracing through the meshes of the canvas.

Now you can do one of two things. First, you can use an *indelible* marker in a neutral shade such as a medium gray, and trace the design on the canvas. Use a marker with a fine tip, or if you cannot get one with a tip that is fine enough, shave yours to a fine point (use a single-edge razor blade). Check the canvas against the tracing and the enlargement for any details you may have missed, and add them carefully. Now, unless you plan to paint in the color scheme, you can follow the color code on the original print.

Or you can outline each section of the design with a sharpened *indelible* marker of the color that is to be used to fill in that specific area. Color right over the medium gray.

If you have large windows, you can tape the tracing of your design to the window, and tape your canvas over the tracing. Just be sure it is on the square with the tracing, and everything is aligned; then proceed as described above. Use a medium gray marker. It is helpful to stand slightly above the design, because the markers work best when the ink flows downward.

This is where you can decide whether or not to paint the canvas. If you do want to—why not? Those German print sellers who began producing painted canvases back in the 1800s weren't the first to draw or color designs on fabric that was to be embroidered. The Chinese were doing it twenty-five centuries ago.

In all honesty, however, I feel I should advise you to go cautiously. Real effort is necessary to develop skill. My attitude about needlepoint is that it should be done for pleasure, and for there to be maximum enjoyment, there should be a minimum of frustration and as few problems as possible.

If you like dabbling with art, or if you have had some training in the use of basic paints and materials, by all means try it. But if you are new to drawing and painting, then consider any painting or art project very carefully. It takes time and sometimes a considerable amount of money and effort to get the materials and art supplies together, and then some practice in order to learn how to use and control the tools and paints. Furthermore, until you've had considerable experience at painting your own work, you may find that when your canvas is stitched, it doesn't look quite the way you had anticipated it would.

Creating a successful needlework design means more than just a beautifully painted picture or even a beautifully painted canvas. It means knowing whether or not the yarn will transmute that beauty in the stitching of the final needlework. So, just as you practiced your stitches on scraps of canvas, it is best to practice on trial pieces before painting your canvas.

Take your original tracing and make another tracing of it. Color this second tracing with crayons or with acrylic paints according to the basic color scheme. Using the colored or painted tracing as your guide, carefully paint the canvas with acrylic paints. *Practice on a piece of scrap canvas first* to be sure that you have thinned the paint sufficiently. You don't want it to clog the meshes; you just want to color the fabric threads of the canvas.

You don't have to match the yarn colors exactly. Just approximate them as best you can, a bit lighter than the yarn color if possible. Avoid using solid black paint on the canvas. It makes it too difficult to see what you are doing. Use a light or medium gray, instead, on those areas where you plan to use black wool. Dead black yarn, incidentally, isn't too satisfactory in needlepoint embroidery; it seems to deaden the color around it. You will be more pleased with black that has an overtone of another hue.

Painting a canvas may seem like unnecessary work when it is relatively easy to follow a graph or an original drawing. It can pay off, though, because yarn seems to color better when it is embroidered over a matching color painted on the canvas. This is especially true of dark colors. If you want to do really fine shading, it is essential that the canvas be painted to indicate the fine gradations.

By the way, though I have mentioned oil paints, waterproof markers, and acrylics for coloring canvas, you may also use colored India inks, which are completely indelible.

Now, how about creating designs of your own? There are several ways of developing original designs, and all kinds of sources of inspiration for designs. All you need to do to get started is to select a motif that entices you enough for you to want to see it in needlepoint. It might be flowers, butterflies, bees, seashells, boats, scenery, medieval drawings, animals, fish—whatever you find interesting. Pictures and ideas exist in abundance all around us. Look in books, magazines, museum shops, card shops, art stores, wallpaper sample books, and catalogs; look at dress and drapery fabrics, at rugs, at architecture. Just one caution. For your first attempt at designing, choose a subject that isn't overly intricate. Try to find one with definite strong outlines and a color scheme that doesn't require too much subtle shading. If you analyze the color codes accompanying the graphs of my designs, you will see that a variety of detail can be achieved with very few colors.

Your design can be an exact copy, or it can be composed of two or three elements from any picture; for example, a wallpaper sample that you think can be rearranged into a pretty pattern for needlepoint.

The first thing to do is trace the design or the sections of the design that interest you. The tracing (or tracings) should then be enlarged by means of photocopying to the size you want the finished design on the canvas to be. If you are going to use the tracing as it is, follow the instructions at the beginning of this chapter for transferring it to a graph or to canvas.

If, however, you want only one of the elements to be large enough to be the major focus of the design, you may want to have that section enlarged and the other sections kept the same size. (When something is photocopied, it can be made larger or smaller than the original.) You might, for instance, select just one element from that wallpaper, have it enlarged, and then have it photocopied in a much reduced size. The enlargement could be the center of the design, with the reduced copies arranged as a border around it. In that way you'd be using the same basic motif in different sizes.

It is now possible to have a color or a black-and-white drawing, painting, or photograph up to 8 x 10 inches put on an iron-on matrix. The service is available from J. C. Nellison, 500 Fifth Avenue, New York, NY 10036. Ask for prices before you order. If you have a very large design, you can have it done in 8 x 10-inch sections and piece them together.

COLOR

Color choices and responses to colors are very personal matters, rooted, perhaps, in past experiences. Most of us tend to react to color much as we do to sound. Just as one kind of music stirs our blood while another calms us, so different colors affect us differently. Some people favor red in all its varieties; others will wear nothing but browns and sunset oranges; and still others always choose a mixture of sea greens and ocean blues. Therefore, although I suggest color schemes for all the designs in this book, if they don't turn you on or if they might clash in the setting you plan for your project, then by all means go your own way and select colors that suit you. It will personalize your work for you and quite possibly lead you into creating designs of your own. Nothing pleases a needlepoint teacher more than that.

Just as fashion has changed and styles have become freewheeling, so have the rules about which colors should go with which. There is much more mixing than matching these days. And after all, if a bright green plant can produce a magenta flower with orange pistils, or if a fish can be deep blue with yellow markings, there is no reason why you can't be as daring as nature is.

Nevertheless, it is instructive to know something about colors and what happens when you mix them, particularly when you want to do some shading or develop a scheme with gradations of tone.

If you've read books on how to paint, or taken some art courses, or read other needlepoint books, what I am about to say won't be new to you. But for those of you for whom needlepoint is a new adventure, these basics may help you when you go to select your yarns.

All colors, all shades, all tones derive from the primary colors: red, yellow, and blue. As one writer has said, "They *are*—they cannot be called into existence by mixing other colors."

The secondary colors are orange, green, and violet. They are made by mixing primaries. Red and blue make violet (or purple). Red and yellow make orange. Yellow and blue make green.

Then there are the tertiary colors. Red and violet, when mixed, become a red violet; red and orange result in a reddish orange; yellow and orange produce an orangey yellow; and so forth. On a color wheel there would be three primary colors, three secondary colors, and six tertiary colors—twelve colors in all.

On the color wheel, the colors opposite each other are called complementary colors. (One way to find the complement of a color is to stare at it without blinking for a minute or two, then close your eyes. You will see its complement cast on the inside of your eyelids for a few seconds.)

The more than 10 million known colors all stem from the three primary colors, and they can all be further altered by the addition of black or white.

True colors are called hues. Tone is the lightness or darkness of a hue. Colors that are identical in tone are almost indistinguishable in a black-and-white photograph. Identical tones are said to have the same value. White is added to a color to make a tone. Adding black will make it a shade.

When a color is mixed with its complement, the result is gray. Since colors of equal tonal value tend to cancel each other out, it is best to avoid putting them next to each other.

Red and the colors that relate to it, such as orange and yellow, are considered warm colors. Blue and its derivatives, purple and green, are called cool. Actually, however, the warmness or coolness of their effect may be accentuated or toned down or even neutralized by the colors adjacent to them. Light colors seem to come forward, and dark ones recede. White is associated with coolness because it tends to repel heat (which is why we wear white or light-colored clothes in the summer), while black and dark colors absorb heat.

Colors vary in effect according to the colors next to them. Complementary colors, for instance, when placed side by side, intensify each other, and grays, when placed near strong primary colors, tend to take on the complementary color cast of those colors.

Pretest your color schemes with crayons or paints on paper. This will give you a good idea of how they will look in needlepoint. And remember, if you embroider a certain color next to another color and the result is ghastly, don't give the project up. Just remove the offending stitches, and try a different color.

The Background Color. When it comes to deciding on a background color for a particular design, two important factors should be considered. First, you will want your piece to fit comfortably in the setting you plan for it. Second, and probably more important, the background should not overwhelm or detract from the design itself. Keep in mind that dark or bright backgrounds have a tendency to make the design appear smaller than it is, whereas pastel shades or subdued colors make the pattern seem more dramatic.

If for any reason you want to use a dark or bright background, then overstitch your design. Overstitching is enlarging the design by adding an extra row or two of stitches to the outline of the pattern. This will compensate for the illusion of a smaller pattern against the background color.

The exact effect of one color against another is unpredictable; it can only be judged after the colors have been stitched and appear next to each other. Holding a hank of yarn of one color against a hank of another color won't do the trick. The best thing is to stitch a row or two around the outer edge of your design. If you feel it's going to work well, then buy enough of the background color to complete your project. If you don't think so, rip it out, enlarge the design, and try again. This may sound like a waste of time, effort, and yarn. But it isn't. Your satisfaction with the finished work will more than compensate for any expenditure caused by reworking the design.

SIX

Some Myths and Fallacies of Needlepoint Lore

FANCY STITCHES

There are many intricate stitches that can be worked on canvas. The best way to learn them, I guess, would be to take a course in canvas stitchery. I don't necessarily discourage the learning of elaborate stitches, but I do feel that the time and money you would spend learning them could be put to better and more satisfying use by working on a beautiful piece of needlepoint.

If the subject matter, the design, the color, and the exactness of detail are the most meaningful aspects of needlework to you—as they are to me—then restrict yourself to the two stitches taught you in this book. They are simple to do, and they produce a surface that won't interfere with the concept or the design or the delicate hues of the Oriental patterns.

Using the complicated stitches that create raised areas and uneven textures requires a very sophisticated artistic ability. Making the texture, or surface variations, the integral element of a design tends to draw attention away from the color and subject. Many of the complicated stitches have a definite shape of their own; in other words, they are textured designs in themselves. The tent stitches taught in this book, on the other hand, are self-effacing and unobtrusive. Elaborate stitches call attention to themselves, to their shapes, their textures. Developing a pattern in which the structural differences in the stitches are as important as the color and the design requires an intuitive sense and a well-trained eye. Knowing where to place particular stitches, what size they should be, and what kinds of stitches relate well to each other takes considerable practice. And there can be many disappointments along the way.

After all, the undisputed masterpieces of needlepoint, past and present, have been done with just the continental and the basketweave stitches.

THE MYTHICAL CIRCLE

You can draw a curve or a circle on a canvas, but there really is no such thing as embroidering a true curve or circle in needlepoint. Instead, your needlepoint creates an *illusion* of a circle. It can't be otherwise, given the physical qualities of canvas which is, after all, made up of tiny squares. The placement of stitches in those squares, following the circular pattern, can create the image of a curved shape. And that, if you analyze it, is exactly what needlepoint is: many small, even bits of color creating a pattern.

BUY CHEAP, PAY DEAR

Beginners are sometimes advised to buy a cheap piece of canvas for a first project. I'm agin it! True, you could ruin a first piece, or discover that needlepoint isn't for you. But you could also find that it is the most fun you've had, and that you love it! In that case, you don't want to risk your money and your learning effort on anything but the best. Needlework is for people who want to make unique and individual objects of the finest quality. A cheap piece of canvas and poor-quality wool may turn you off by their very cheapness. Cheap canvas is usually synthetic and unpleasant to work on. Cheap yarns are often made of acrylic or some other synthetic fiber without the life and the springiness that natural fibers have. Cheap canvas is probably poorly printed, so the finished canvas—if you finish it—bears little resemblance to the picture on the package. Instead of buying cheap, watch for sales in stores and shops that sell quality canvases. Then, for the same price, you'll end up with something you can be proud of.

Just be sure that your first effort is fairly simple and not too large. A piece about 12 to 14 inches square is about right for a start.

THE ONE-COLOR-AT-A-TIME RULE

If anything can make needlepoint boring, it's the notion that you have to complete all the areas that require one color before you can start the other colors. In addition to being tedious, this procedure has you holding bulky, finished canvas in your hand almost from the start, which is not only uncomfortable but can cause unnecessary soiling. Instead, as I suggested earlier, start from the center and go outward, or— and I personally prefer this—do the upper-right-hand area, including the background, then complete the entire right side, and then do the upper-left-hand segment. By leaving the lower left portion for last, you will find that the canvas is easier to hold. This system is particularly good for large pieces; the unfinished area and the part you are working on can be on your lap, and the rest rolled up, out of the way.

DOES A LARGE PIECE TAKE TOO LONG?

If you have already done quite a lot of needlepoint but have shied away from doing something really big and impressive because you think it will take too long, turn your thinking around. First, imagine how beautiful it will look and how accomplished you and your friends will think you are. In other words, to quote a friend of mine, "Keep your eye on the star, not on the steps to it." Then approach the time problem by thinking about it this way. How many small pieces did you do during the past six months? Perhaps three? What size were they? If these pieces were put together, would they make a rug? If so, then a rug could be done in the same amount of time.

Or look at it like this. Take the average number of lengths of wool you usually stitch in an hour. The average is about five. Five strands of yarn cover about five square inches. Calculate the square inches of the rug you'd like to make, divide that by five, and you have the number of hours it will take to complete the rug or other large piece.

For example, say a rug is 3 feet by 4 feet, which is 12 square feet, or 1,728 square inches. Divide 1,728 square inches by 5, which is how many square inches you do in an hour. It equals 345. Therefore, if you averaged an hour a day, you would finish the rug in less than a year.

So forget your fear of big things. The rug will be done before you know it!

THE UNFINISHED PIECE

If there is one thing you should never worry or feel guilty about, it is an unfinished canvas. Much of the pleasure of needlepoint is in the relaxing effect of the stitching itself, so don't ever rush yourself. If you just enjoy the simple rhythm of putting the needle and wool through the canvas and admire each emerging small detail of the design, the work will get completed without your even thinking about it. When you start a large project, or even a small one, don't put a target date on finishing. Instead, anticipate the months—or years—of enchantment and pleasure ahead.

NEEDLEPOINT IS GOOD EXERCISE

Don't feel that because you are just sitting quietly and enjoying your needlepoint, you aren't getting the exercise you think you need. You are. And if you can just learn to sit in the lotus position while stitching, not only will your body become strong, but your soul will expand along with your art. Seriously, needlepoint *is* good exercise. It strengthens your shoulders, arms, and pectoral muscles. You just don't feel any exertion while doing it.

NEW PLEASURES COME IN DIFFERENT SIZES

One of the fascinating and delightful aspects of needlepoint embroidery is to discover the quality and quantity of detail that simple stitches can achieve on the different mesh sizes of canvas. For instance, a 10-mesh mono canvas has 100 stitches to the square inch, but a 14-mesh canvas will accommodate nearly twice as many, or 196 stitches to the square inch. An 18-mesh canvas allows for 324 stitches to the square inch, while 12-mesh allows for 144 stitches. Penelope canvases, of course, offer the possibility of adding even more stitches, as well as great variety in the size of stitches.

If you have worked mostly on largish mesh, such as #10 canvas, I urge you to try petit point. It is more intimate, and its potential for meticulous rendering of fine detail and elegant shading will provide you with a whole new experience.

But if you have been working exclusively on very small mesh canvases or on petit point, then encountering 10-mesh and larger canvases will be a revelation and a true joy. It's relaxing—a little like taking off a tight piece of clothing. The patterns actually seem to paint themselves.

Needlepointers are artists. And just as artists experiment with different-sized brushes, so needlepointers should learn what can be done on a large variety of mesh-size canvases. Be adventurous. Explore various yarn plies, different needles, and untried color combinations. You'll discover a rich new world of beauty and excitement.

SEVEN

Oriental Designs with Graph Patterns

BATS WITH CLOUDS

The early Chinese worshiped nature and attached symbolic significance to many animals, trees, and flowers. They felt that certain animals not only embodied admirable character traits but could somehow transfer these qualities to people. They would have one or more of these animals depicted on items intended as gifts in order to send (or wish) the appropriate animal characteristics on to the receivers.

Some animals, flowers, and plants acquired their symbolic significance by virtue of being homonyms; that is, the name of a particular flower or animal suggested another word having a similar sound which meant something good. For instance, in Chinese *lu* means deer; the sound *lu* also means income from an official position. So a deer stands for a comfortable living, or status. And if you give someone a gift with the picture of a deer on it, you are in fact wishing the person prosperity or success. The bat is a very popular symbol in Chinese art. It has none of the connotations of evil that it has for us. On the contrary, the word for bat, *fu*, is a homonym for happiness. A group of five bats, as in this design, symbolizes the five blessings: longevity, wealth, serenity, virtue, and easy death.

When worked on 18-mesh mono canvas, this design will measure 10 inches by 12 inches. Cut a piece of canvas 14 inches by 16 inches, and bind the edges.

THE PATERNAYAN COLORS ARE:

242   RED (*inside wings*)

978   LIGHT ORANGE (*inside wings*)

968   ORANGE (*inside wings*)

452   YELLOW (*outside wings, head*)

752   BLUE (*wings*)

597   GREEN (*clouds*)

594   LIGHT SILVER GREEN (*clouds*)

506   BLACK GREEN (*background, eyes*)

FISH WITH SUN

This fish was inspired by an antique porcelain plate. The fish is one of the most common subjects of Chinese painting and embroidery, probably because fishing has always been so popular in the coastal areas of China. Fishing requires sitting still and waiting for a bite; it therefore lends itself to meditation and contemplation. This seems to make it an ideal pastime for scholars and people who enjoy silence and solitude.

When worked on 10-mesh mono canvas, this design will measure 16 inches in diameter. Cut a piece of canvas 20 inches by 20 inches, and bind the edges.

THE PATERNAYAN COLORS ARE:

354 LIGHT GREEN (*background*)

455 BEIGE GOLD (*clouds, tail, head*)

G64 BRIGHT GREEN (*body, fins*)

005 WHITE (*scales, top of waves*)

389 GRAY (*scales*)

346 DARK GRAY (*scales*)

108 CHARCOAL (*scales*)

968 ORANGE (*sun*)

G30 TURQUOISE (*waves*)

G28 DARK TURQUOISE (*waves*)

506 BLACK GREEN (*waves*)

452 YELLOW (*whiskers, tail*)

FISH WITH SUN

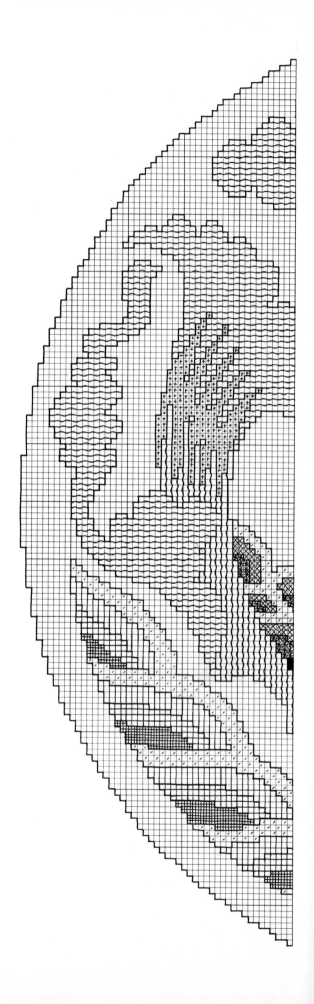

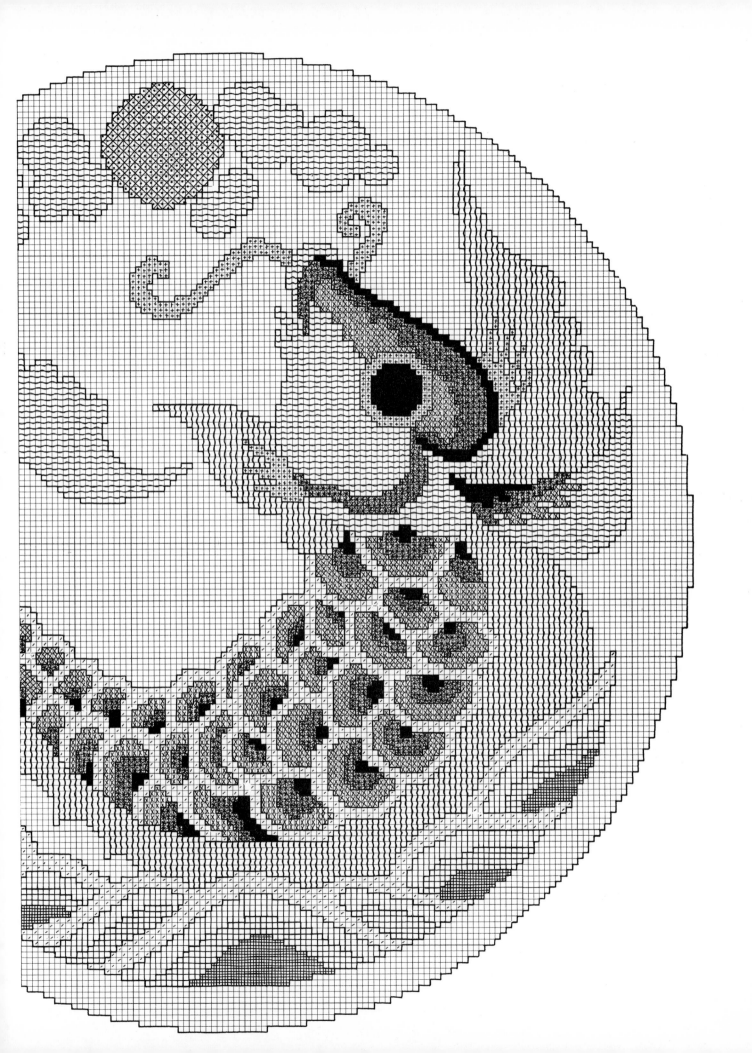

PEACH TREE WITH ROCKS

The peach tree has been rivaled in popularity only by the flowering plum as inspiration for the legend makers, poets, and artists of China. Tree, flower, fruit, and seed all have special symbolic meaning. The tree itself is said to frighten away demons, and its blossoms are particularly feared by evil spirits. The seed is a protective amulet for children, and cradles are made of peach wood to ward off harmful goblins. When the peach tree blooms, it is time to arrange marriages; and the fruit is then made into wine for the wedding feast. The peaches themselves symbolize the essence of woman. "To go into the peach garden" means to consummate a love affair.

In needlework compositions, the Chinese seldom depict trees alone. They place them in a naturalistic setting, with outcroppings of rock to stabilize the angular grace of the branches, and, sometimes, with water and clouds to complement the color of the fruit or the blossoms.

When worked on 14-mesh mono canvas, this design will measure 16 inches by 16 inches. Cut a piece of canvas 20 inches by 20 inches, and bind the edges.

THE PATERNAYAN COLORS ARE:

496	PALE BEIGE	*(background)*
001	WHITE	*(fruit)*
860	LIGHT PINK	*(fruit, flowers)*
855	DARK PINK	*(fruit, flowers)*
168	LIGHT GRAY	*(rock)*
162	DARK GRAY	*(tree)*
436	PALE TERRA COTTA	*(mushroom)*
416	LIGHT TERRA COTTA	*(mushroom)*
620	LIGHT VIOLET	*(mushroom)*
615	DARK VIOLET	*(mushroom)*
570	LIGHT GREEN	*(leaves, rock)*
575	VERY LIGHT GREEN	*(ground, rock)*
527	GREEN	*(grass, line in rock)*
504	DARK GREEN	*(leaves)*
020	LIGHT TAN	*(ground)*
535	MEDIUM TURQUOISE	*(ground)*
395	LIGHT BLUE	*(rock)*
385	MEDIUM BLUE	*(rock, line in rock)*
025	DARK TAN	*(mushroom)*
123	DARK TAUPE	*(tree)*

PEACH TREE WITH ROCKS

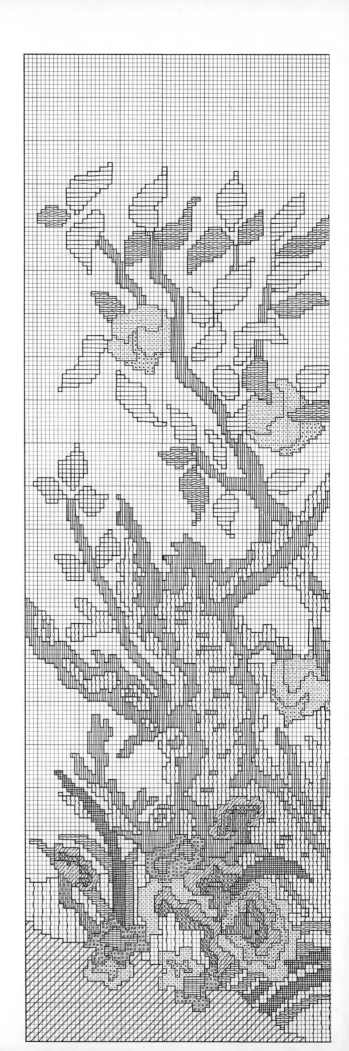

DRAGON BELLPULL

The dragon is a familiar motif in Chinese art, but it is not of Chinese origin or invention. As far as we know, the earliest rendition of a dragon appeared in the art of Mesopotamia, in the Middle East, at least 2,000 years before it was seen in the art of China. The first known Chinese dragon was created during the Shang era, about 1500 B.C. Art historians have found evidence of both Iranian and Mesopotamian influences in early Chinese art, so it seems safe to say that that is where Chinese dragons emigrated from.

Stories about dragons exist in nearly every recorded civilization and date from very early times. Descriptions of dragons vary somewhat, especially in the small details. The Chinese dragon, according to one authority, is supposed to have more or less the head of a horse, the tail of a snake, wings on its sides, and four legs. Each of the four feet has four claws, except on the imperial dragon, which has five claws on each foot. The dragon of China differs from Western dragons, called chimeras, in that the Chinese dragon isn't considered an evil force but a good one. Because the Chinese dragon is an animal of the sky and represents clouds, rain, and lightning, it ensures the fertility of the fields and a good harvest. As a benevolent force, it became the emblem of high government officials and, ultimately, the insignia of the emperors.

When worked on 14-mesh mono canvas, this design will measure 10 inches by 45 inches. Cut a piece of canvas 14 inches by 49 inches, and bind the edges.

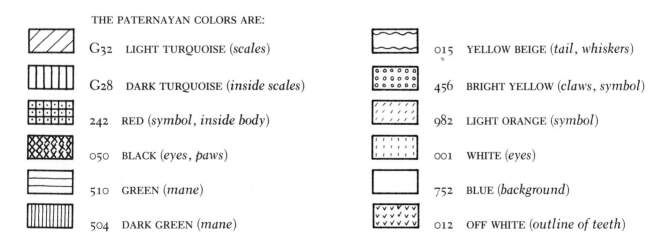

THE PATERNAYAN COLORS ARE:

G32   LIGHT TURQUOISE (*scales*)

G28   DARK TURQUOISE (*inside scales*)

242   RED (*symbol, inside body*)

050   BLACK (*eyes, paws*)

510   GREEN (*mane*)

504   DARK GREEN (*mane*)

015   YELLOW BEIGE (*tail, whiskers*)

456   BRIGHT YELLOW (*claws, symbol*)

982   LIGHT ORANGE (*symbol*)

001   WHITE (*eyes*)

752   BLUE (*background*)

012   OFF WHITE (*outline of teeth*)

DRAGON BELLPULL

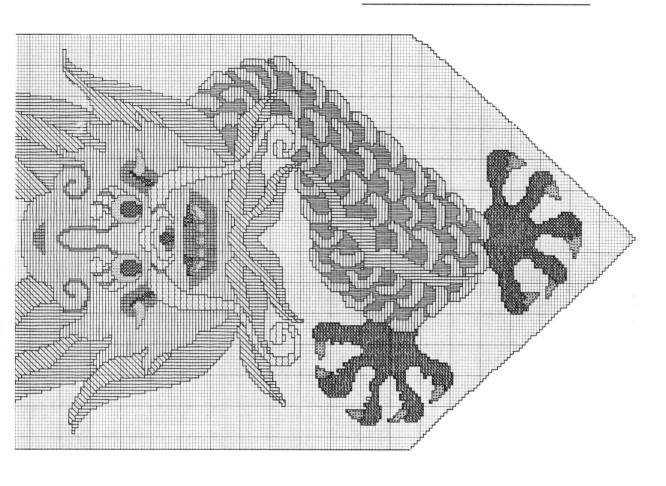

DRAGON BOAT

Beneficent as the Chinese dragon is supposed to have been, it was not without a temper befitting its ferocious appearance. As controller of rain clouds, the dragon could become destructive and pour flooding rains on the fields and make the rivers rise out of their banks. The early Chinese thought thunderstorms and tempests were dragons fighting with each other. Consequently, they made sure to treat dragons with respect and to keep them happy with an occasional sacrifice. In modern times a symbolic offering is still made to a play dragon on Chinese New Year.

Among the ceremonies that have come down from ancient times is the Dragon Festival, held on the fifth day of the fifth month of every year. In Chinese communities where there are rivers or other navigable waters, the people build boats resembling dragons and have dragon boat races. They pull the boats ashore at the end of the festival and burn them as a symbolic sacrifice.

This dragon boat contains an amusing arrangement of little houses.

When worked on 14-mesh mono canvas, this design will measure 14 inches by 18 inches. Cut a piece of canvas 18 inches by 22 inches, and bind the edges. Add additional canvas for larger area.

THE PATERNAYAN COLORS ARE:

010	CREAM	(*background*)
001	WHITE	(*outlines of houses, doorways*)
427	GOLD	(*body of dragon*)
467	YELLOW	(*houses*)
131	GREEN BROWN	(*dragon's scales, chimneys*)
860	LIGHT PINK	(*oars, inside body of dragon, roof*)
850	DARK PINK	(*outline and trim on houses, body and mouth of dragon*)
395	LIGHT BLUE	(*waves, trim and roofs of houses, eyebrows and body of dragon*)
330	DARK BLUE	(*outlines of houses, body and eyes of dragon*)

DRAGON BOAT

FIRE SCREEN WITH SIX VASES OF FLOWERS
PAGE 91

PIANO BENCH COVER WITH TWO DRAGONS
PAGE 67

DRAGON BOAT
PAGE 63

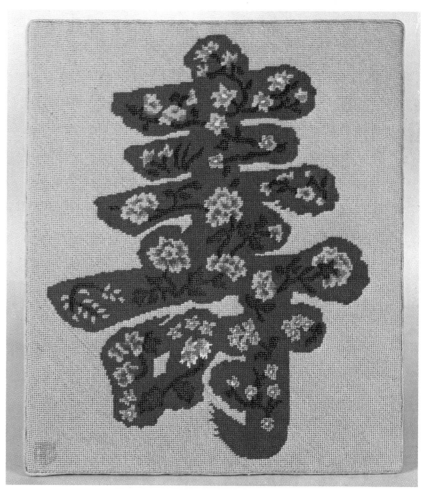

CALLIGRAPHY DESIGN: LONGEVITY
PAGE 115

BLUE CRANE
PAGE 119

SCENE WITH WATER AND HOUSES
PAGE 99

FLOWERING BRANCH
PAGE 75

PHOENIXES ON AN IMARI PLATE
PAGE 87

BLUE CARP PLATE
PAGE 79

BAT MEDALLION
PAGE 111

FISH WITH SUN
PAGE 51

DRAGON BELLPULL
PAGE 59

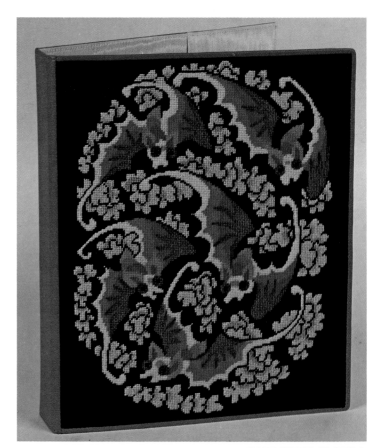

BATS WITH CLOUDS
PAGE 47

LANDSCAPE WITH MOUNTAINS, HOUSES, AND CLOUDS
PAGE 95

JAPANESE WOMAN
PAGE 103

JAPANESE MAN
PAGE 107

TWO BIRDS ON A FLOWERING BRANCH
PAGE 83

PEACH TREE WITH ROCKS
PAGE 55

BATS—SYMMETRICAL DESIGN
PAGE 123

THE DOG OF FO
PAGE 71

PIANO BENCH COVER WITH TWO DRAGONS

Chinese folklore has it that one of the ancestors of the Hsia dynasty transformed himself into a dragon. Another tale relates that one branch of the Hsia family knew how to breed dragons. Still another tells that a certain Hsia ruler ate dragons so that his reign would be a prosperous one. Dragons were also thought to be the forefathers of *all* emperors.

When the emperors of China adopted the dragon as their official symbol, they had it embroidered on their imperial robes and painted on the objects of their household. Many artists who specialized in the painting of dragons became well known. Soame Jenyns in his book *A Background to Chinese Painting* quotes one of these painters, T'ang Yung, who said, "If you want to make them, with sweeping brush and flowing ink bring out the life of the muscles and bones; but in order to express perfectly the essence and spirit of the dragon, you must give him awe-inspiring bloody eyes, impetuously moving red beard, mist-hoarding scales, bristling mane, hair on the knees, claws and teeth . . . make him skip and gambol as he soars through space. . . ."

The dragon in China is the official keeper of one of the four directions—east. Dragons also guard forbidden treasure, and the Chinese dragon is often shown chasing a pearl, which in Chinese mythology has cosmic significance.

When worked on 14-mesh mono canvas, this design will measure 15 inches by 18 inches. Cut a piece of canvas 19 inches by 22 inches, and bind the edges.

Repeat the graph on the canvas as two mirror images, and carry through the pattern of the hills on the bottom according to the size of your bench.

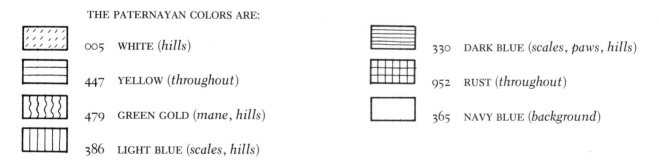

THE PATERNAYAN COLORS ARE:

005   WHITE (*hills*)

447   YELLOW (*throughout*)

479   GREEN GOLD (*mane, hills*)

386   LIGHT BLUE (*scales, hills*)

330   DARK BLUE (*scales, paws, hills*)

952   RUST (*throughout*)

365   NAVY BLUE (*background*)

PIANO BENCH

COVER WITH

TWO DRAGONS

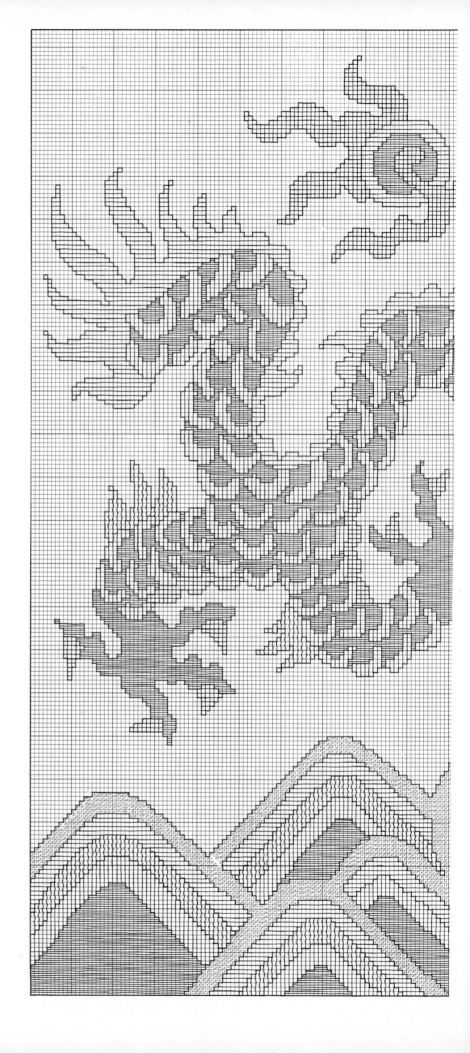

THE DOG OF FO

That fanciful ceramic animal that looks a little like an outsize Pekingese and is called a Fo dog by collectors of Chinese antiquities isn't a dog at all; it is a lion.

Lions are not native to China. They were brought in during the Han era as a gift or tribute. But for centuries they were so rare that artists treated them more often as fable than as fact.

Lions entered Chinese art from two directions. From the north, they came as the favorite motif of the invading Scythians who taught the Chinese artisans to portray lions naturalistically in decorations on their ceramic jars. And when the Buddhists of India came from the East to spread their religion through China, the stylized lions that were part of Indian decor traveled with the religious groups to serve as guardians of the temple doors. It was thus that they earned their name, Dogs of Fo, Fo meaning Buddha.

Sometimes Fo dogs were used to decorate temple altars; others were placed in the courtyards of magistrates as symbols of justice and of the dignity of the law. Their fierce expression was supposed to frighten away devils and other evil spirits.

Much of its ferociousness is tamed into charm when the Fo dog is captured in needlepoint.

When worked on 14-mesh mono canvas, this design will measure 16 inches by 16 inches. Cut a piece of canvas 20 inches by 20 inches, and bind the edges.

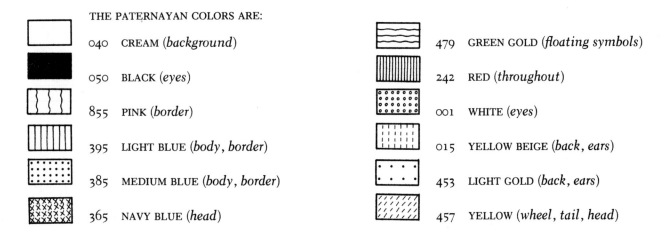

THE PATERNAYAN COLORS ARE:

040   CREAM (*background*)

050   BLACK (*eyes*)

855   PINK (*border*)

395   LIGHT BLUE (*body, border*)

385   MEDIUM BLUE (*body, border*)

365   NAVY BLUE (*head*)

479   GREEN GOLD (*floating symbols*)

242   RED (*throughout*)

001   WHITE (*eyes*)

015   YELLOW BEIGE (*back, ears*)

453   LIGHT GOLD (*back, ears*)

457   YELLOW (*wheel, tail, head*)

THE DOG OF FO

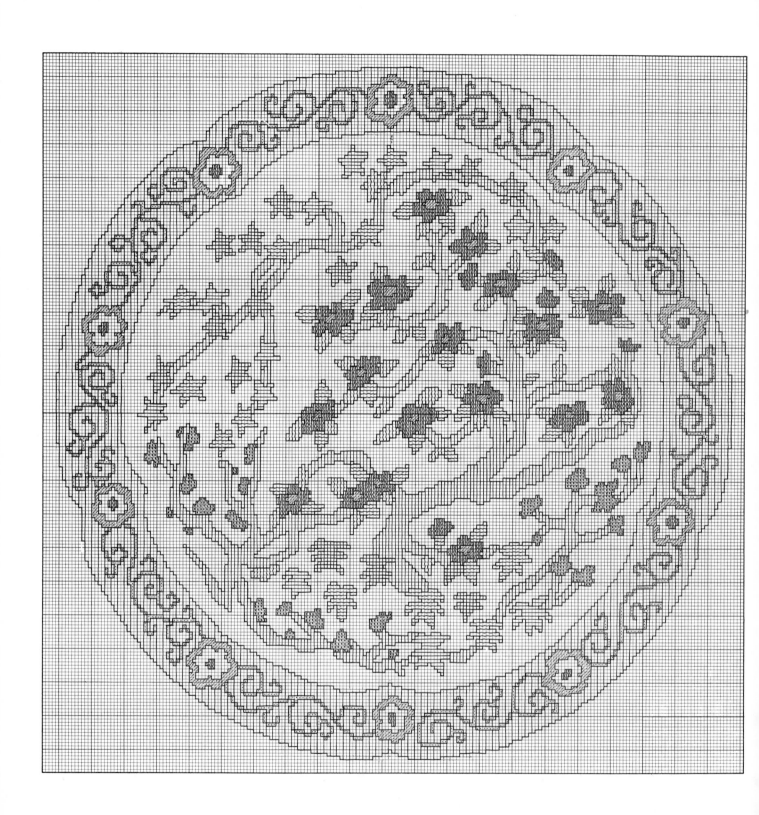

FLOWERING BRANCH

This design taken from a piece of antique embroidered silk is further evidence of the intense love the Chinese have for flowers. They use them on every possible occasion. Certain flowers represent the seasons; others are associated with festivals or are endowed with characteristics human beings should hope to develop.

The plum blossom, for instance, which begins to appear on the bare bark of the tree even before the last snows have melted away, represents endurance. It shows that the tree has lived through the winter and can greet the spring.

Because of its delicacy, the plum blossom also symbolizes female beauty; many Chinese girls have been named Plum Blossom by wishful and well-meaning parents. The winter plum tree and its blooms have been the subject of many poems and philosophical treatises. The plum tree is rivaled only by the peach tree as a subject of painting, poetry, and embroidery. It is also a popular motif for porcelain vases and bowls.

When worked on 14-mesh mono canvas, this design will measure 16 inches by 16 inches. Cut a piece of canvas 20 inches by 20 inches, and bind the edges.

THE PATERNAYAN COLORS ARE:

512   DARK SILVER GREEN (*tree*)

560   SILVER GREEN (LEAVES)

242   RED (*flowers*)

457   YELLOW (*flowers*)

810   MAROON (*border*)

133   TAUPE (*border*)

860   LIGHT PINK (*flowers*)

G74   LIGHT GREEN (*leaves*)

479   GREEN GOLD (*leaves*)

542   LIGHT GREEN (*leaves*)

001   WHITE (*background*)

FLOWERING BRANCH

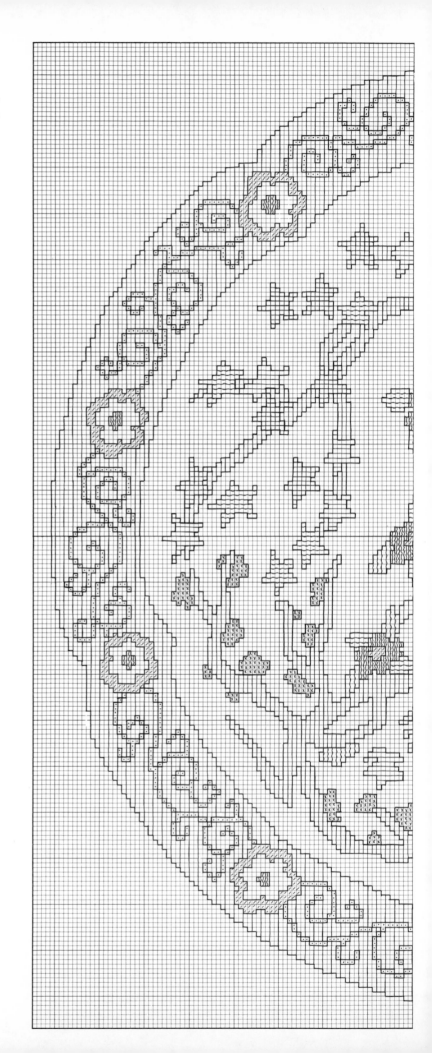

BLUE CARP PLATE

There is hardly a culture or religion that doesn't include fish in its symbology, and the religions of China and Japan are no exception. In China, the word for fish, *yu*, is a homonym for another word *yu*, which means superfluity or extreme luxury. The fish, then, stands for abundance, and for nature's capacity to reproduce. Because fish never sleep, they are also a symbol of vigilance. And because they can move so easily in water, they represent freedom.

The carp is probably China's most revered fish. As a large goldfish, it is a favorite object of art. It is also a favorite table delicacy.

When carp are ready to spawn, they swim up the Yangtze River and the other great rivers of China. According to ancient belief, if they manage to leap the cataracts and swim the rapids, they become dragons. Hence, the carp also stands for energy, strength, perseverance, and achievement.

When worked on 14-mesh mono canvas, this design will measure 16 inches by 16 inches. Cut a piece of canvas 20 inches by 20 inches, and bind the edges.

THE PATERNAYAN COLORS ARE:

001 WHITE (*inside border, background*)

743 LIGHT BLUE (*center motif, symbols in border*)

741 MEDIUM BLUE (*center motif*)

G30 TURQUOISE (*outside border*)

365 NAVY BLUE (*outside border*)

242 RED (*outside border*)

427 GOLD (*borders*)

452 YELLOW (*symbols in outside border*)

BLUE CARP PLATE

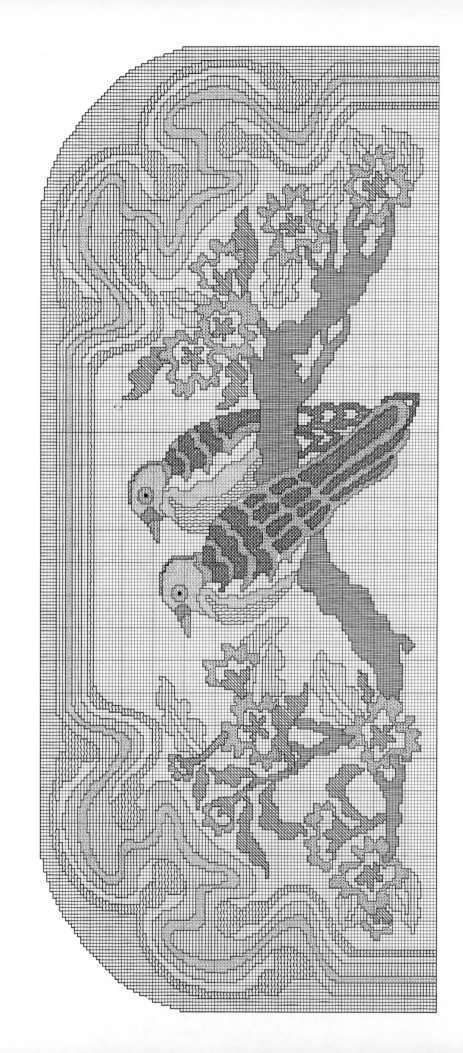

TWO BIRDS ON A FLOWERING BRANCH

The Chinese did not *always* attach a symbolic meaning to every painting. These two birds on a flowering branch come from a work that was very obviously done out of sheer love of nature. The decorative border, however, derives from a Chinese design that suggests both sky and water.

When worked on 14-mesh mono canvas, this design will measure 9 inches by 21½ inches. Cut a piece of canvas 13 inches by 25½ inches, and bind the edges.

THE PATERNAYAN COLORS ARE:

050   BLACK (*eyes*)

334   DARK BLUE (*feathers of birds*)

385   MEDIUM BLUE (*border, leaves*)

395   LIGHT BLUE (*feathers of birds*)

396   VERY LIGHT BLUE (*border*)

131   GREEN BROWN (*branch*)

479   GREEN GOLD (*leaves*)

457   YELLOW (*flowers, beaks*)

133   MEDIUM TAUPE (*border, birds*)

143   LIGHT TAUPE (*border, birds*)

001   WHITE (*background, birds*)

025   DARK TAN (*border*)

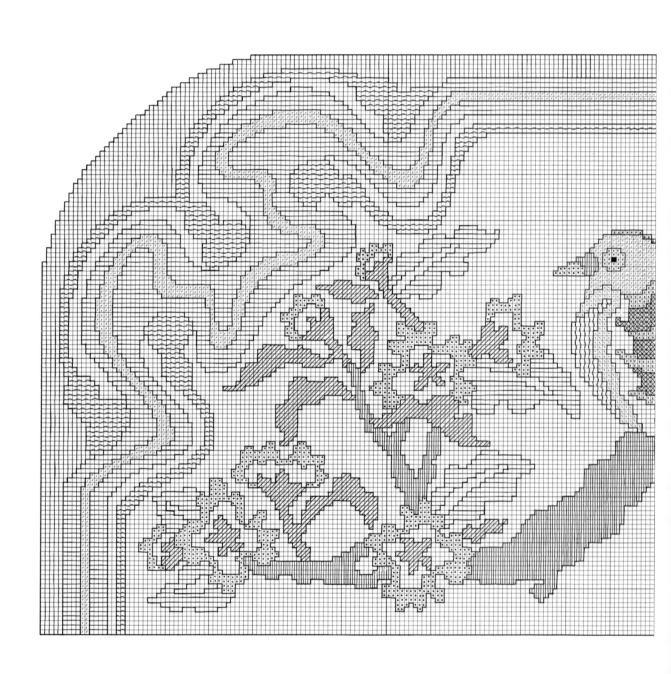

PHOENIXES ON AN IMARI PLATE

Although the Japanese learned much of the art of ceramics and porcelain from the Chinese, they proved themselves capable innovators and soon developed styles and designs that were distinctly and unmistakably Japanese. In fact, at one point the Chinese actually began borrowing from the Japanese! The most famous example of this is the well-known Imari ware. Imari was originally made by the Japanese late in the seventeenth century and was named for the town of Imari because the ceramics first came from there. The Chinese began imitating the porcelain and the Japanese designs on it for their overseas markets. The pattern became so popular in the West that European pottery companies then began imitating the Chinese copies! As a result, innumerable versions as well as detailed copies of Imari spread throughout the world. The imitations were characterized by rather strong colors not generally characteristic of the Chinese.

To me this Imari plate with the Chinese phoenixes flying around is quite charming. The phoenix is rather unglamorously referred to as the heavenly chicken. The dragon of birds, it has the wattles of a cock, the curling neck plumage of the Mandarin teal, legs with rooster spurs, and toes like a parrot. When it appears, says old Chinese legend, there will be peace everywhere in the land.

When worked on 14-mesh mono canvas, this design will measure 16 inches in diameter. Cut a piece of canvas 20 inches by 20 inches, and bind the edges.

THE PATERNAYAN COLORS ARE:

001   WHITE (*background, outside border*)

G30   TURQUOISE (*outside border*)

G28   DARK TURQUOISE (*tiny lines in border*)

242   RED (*border, bird in center*)

452   YELLOW (*outside border*)

427   GOLD (*throughout*)

011   PALE LAVENDER (*background of inner circle*)

395   LIGHT BLUE (*throughout*)

385   MEDIUM BLUE (*throughout*)

855   PINK (*center flowers, bird*)

PHOENIXES ON AN IMARI PLATE

FIRE SCREEN WITH SIX VASES OF FLOWERS

On this screen, the blossoms, foliage, and drifting branches of a serene Oriental garden have been brought indoors. Though the branches and blossoms are in vases, the studied casualness of the arrangement endows them with the same natural rhythm they would have if they were still outside. Some of the rugged outdoor setting that would be the natural home of the delicate flowers is retained in the plant stands which are made of raw burls of wood.

The combination of flowers may have a special meaning, for the Chinese were fond of forming rebuses by means of juxtaposing plants of special significance into floral arrangements, but in this instance the composition needs no further significance than the fact of its charm.

When worked on 12-mesh mono canvas, this design will measure 22½ inches by 30 inches. Cut a piece of canvas 26½ inches by 34 inches, and bind the edges.

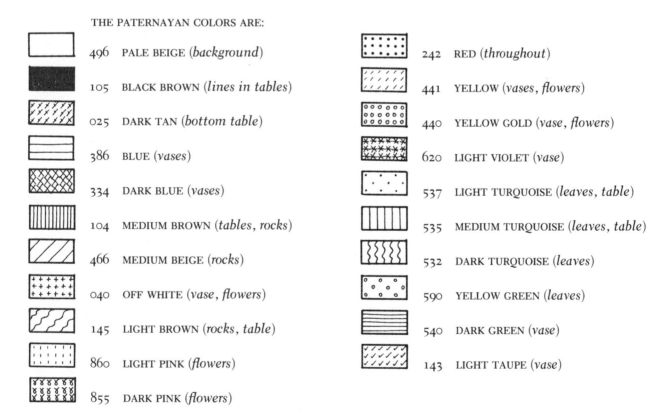

THE PATERNAYAN COLORS ARE:

496   PALE BEIGE (*background*)

105   BLACK BROWN (*lines in tables*)

025   DARK TAN (*bottom table*)

386   BLUE (*vases*)

334   DARK BLUE (*vases*)

104   MEDIUM BROWN (*tables, rocks*)

466   MEDIUM BEIGE (*rocks*)

040   OFF WHITE (*vase, flowers*)

145   LIGHT BROWN (*rocks, table*)

860   LIGHT PINK (*flowers*)

855   DARK PINK (*flowers*)

242   RED (*throughout*)

441   YELLOW (*vases, flowers*)

440   YELLOW GOLD (*vase, flowers*)

620   LIGHT VIOLET (*vase*)

537   LIGHT TURQUOISE (*leaves, table*)

535   MEDIUM TURQUOISE (*leaves, table*)

532   DARK TURQUOISE (*leaves*)

590   YELLOW GREEN (*leaves*)

540   DARK GREEN (*vase*)

143   LIGHT TAUPE (*vase*)

FIRE SCREEN

WITH SIX VASES

OF FLOWERS

LANDSCAPE WITH MOUNTAINS, HOUSES, AND CLOUDS

Early Chinese landscape painters were amazingly skillful. Art historian Soame Jenyns says in A Background to Chinese Painting that they were able to "heap" a great number of scenic devices together in one composition and still create harmony. "Mountains rise sheer from plains . . . trees tangled with creepers hang over precipices, monasteries are perched high above rivers that surge through gorges below. . . ." The reasons for this can perhaps be found in a difference between Eastern and Western attitudes about nature. European painters like to portray nature as a tamed provider, governed by the farmer and the plow. The vast landscape of China is generally more hostile than that, with vast deserts, barren mountain ranges, and huge swamps. The places where nature is hospitable have traditionally been sought out as retreats by retiring priests, politicians, poets, and artists wanting to follow the Taoist and Buddhist precept that living with nature is the way to spiritual enlightenment.

However, "though impatient to enjoy a life amidst the luxuries of nature," Soame Jenyns quotes from Sei-ichi Taki, "most people are debarred from indulging in such pleasures. To meet this want, artists have endeavored to represent landscapes of nature that people may be able to behold the grandeur . . . without stepping out of their houses. . . ."

When worked on 14-mesh mono canvas, this design will measure 16 inches by 16 inches. Cut a piece of canvas 20 inches by 20 inches, and bind the edges.

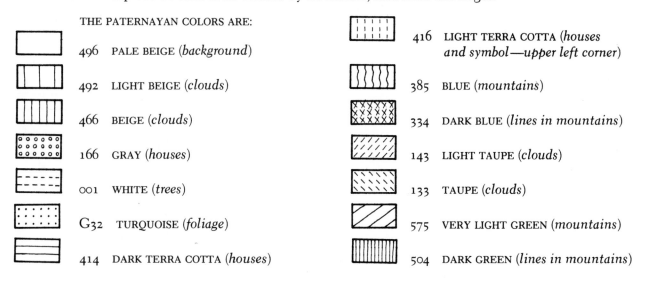

THE PATERNAYAN COLORS ARE:

496   PALE BEIGE (*background*)

492   LIGHT BEIGE (*clouds*)

466   BEIGE (*clouds*)

166   GRAY (*houses*)

001   WHITE (*trees*)

G32   TURQUOISE (*foliage*)

414   DARK TERRA COTTA (*houses*)

416   LIGHT TERRA COTTA (*houses and symbol—upper left corner*)

385   BLUE (*mountains*)

334   DARK BLUE (*lines in mountains*)

143   LIGHT TAUPE (*clouds*)

133   TAUPE (*clouds*)

575   VERY LIGHT GREEN (*mountains*)

504   DARK GREEN (*lines in mountains*)

LANDSCAPE WITH MOUNTAINS, HOUSES, AND CLOUDS

SCENE WITH WATER AND HOUSES

Scenes like this were almost as likely to be "painted" with silk thread on a silk ground as with watercolors on paper. They are traditional in concept, though they may differ in detail, and their beauty comes in great part from the artist's imagination. They are not necessarily typical of the general terrain of China. But, writes Soame Jenyns in *A Background to Chinese Painting*, such scenes are "the scenery that the Chinese most admire, and as they never paint landscapes from nature, their imaginations find fuller range in the impenetrable mountains and forests of their distant provinces."

Jenyns quotes the Chinese writer Wang Wei who wrote over fifteen hundred years ago: "To gaze upon the clouds in autumn, a soaring exaltation in the soul; to feel the spring breeze stirring wild exultant thoughts—what is there in the possession of gold and jewels to compare with delights like these? And then to unroll the portfolio, spread the silk and transfer to it the glories of flood and feel the green forest, the blowing winds, the white water . . . these are the joys of painting."

They are also some of the joys of needlepoint art.

When worked on 14-mesh mono canvas, this design will measure 16 inches by 16 inches. Cut a piece of canvas 20 inches by 20 inches, and bind the edges.

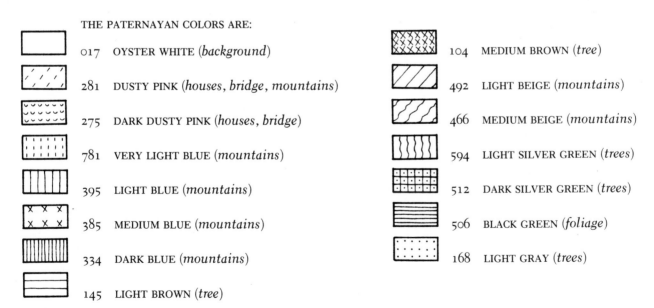

THE PATERNAYAN COLORS ARE:

017 OYSTER WHITE (*background*)

281 DUSTY PINK (*houses, bridge, mountains*)

275 DARK DUSTY PINK (*houses, bridge*)

781 VERY LIGHT BLUE (*mountains*)

395 LIGHT BLUE (*mountains*)

385 MEDIUM BLUE (*mountains*)

334 DARK BLUE (*mountains*)

145 LIGHT BROWN (*tree*)

104 MEDIUM BROWN (*tree*)

492 LIGHT BEIGE (*mountains*)

466 MEDIUM BEIGE (*mountains*)

594 LIGHT SILVER GREEN (*trees*)

512 DARK SILVER GREEN (*trees*)

506 BLACK GREEN (*foliage*)

168 LIGHT GRAY (*trees*)

SCENE WITH WATER
AND HOUSES

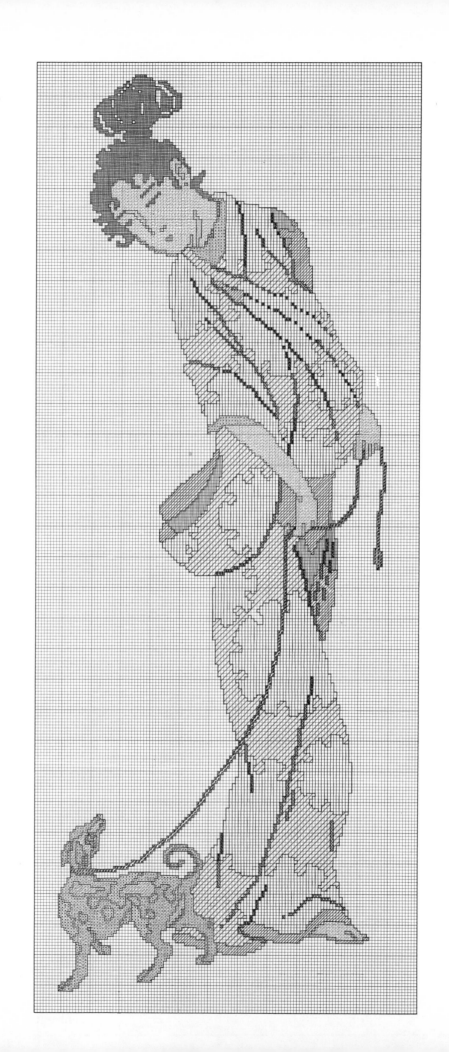

JAPANESE WOMAN

This figure is from a very famous work known in Japan as the Hikone Screen. The actual date of its painting is not known, but it has been owned for several generations by the Ito family, and since the middle of the seventeenth century, it has been considered as a masterpiece of its kind.

The woman I have chosen is only one of the figures in a lively scene showing a man and a woman playing checkers. In the original another woman is watching them, and a young man is playing the samisen, a three-stringed wooden instrument something like a banjo. From her kimono, we can tell that this young woman is a servant. The kimono was an adaptation of the kind of clothes the Chinese were wearing during the P'ang dynasty. Loose and comfortable, it became a popular garment, with designs and even whole scenes woven, painted, or embroidered on the fabric. There were class or status restrictions on the quality of the fabric and on the patterns. The most beautiful silks were worn only by the nobility and those with great wealth.

When worked on 14-mesh mono canvas, this design will measure 9 inches by 22 inches. Cut a piece of canvas 13 inches by 26 inches, and bind the edges.

Hint: Stitch the lines in the kimono with single strands of yarn to create very fine lines.

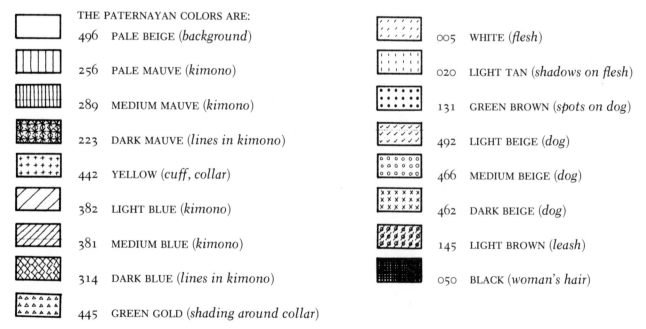

THE PATERNAYAN COLORS ARE:

496   PALE BEIGE (*background*)

256   PALE MAUVE (*kimono*)

289   MEDIUM MAUVE (*kimono*)

223   DARK MAUVE (*lines in kimono*)

442   YELLOW (*cuff, collar*)

382   LIGHT BLUE (*kimono*)

381   MEDIUM BLUE (*kimono*)

314   DARK BLUE (*lines in kimono*)

445   GREEN GOLD (*shading around collar*)

005   WHITE (*flesh*)

020   LIGHT TAN (*shadows on flesh*)

131   GREEN BROWN (*spots on dog*)

492   LIGHT BEIGE (*dog*)

466   MEDIUM BEIGE (*dog*)

462   DARK BEIGE (*dog*)

145   LIGHT BROWN (*leash*)

050   BLACK (*woman's hair*)

JAPANESE WOMAN

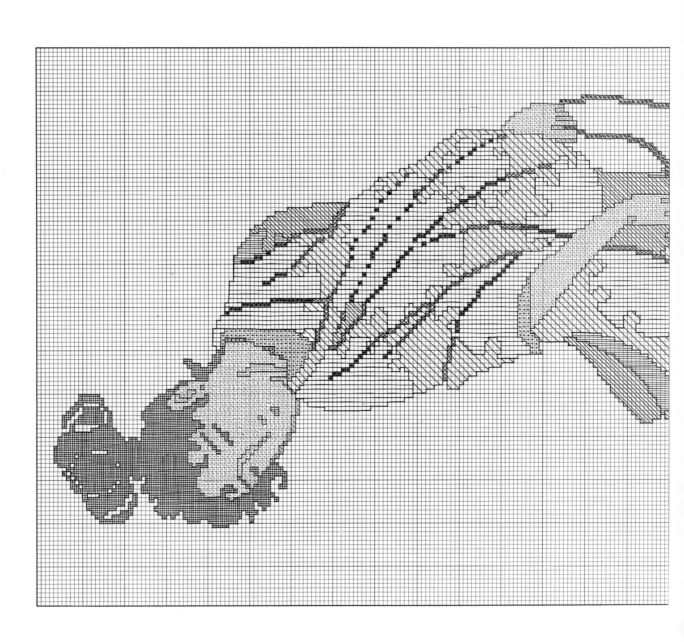

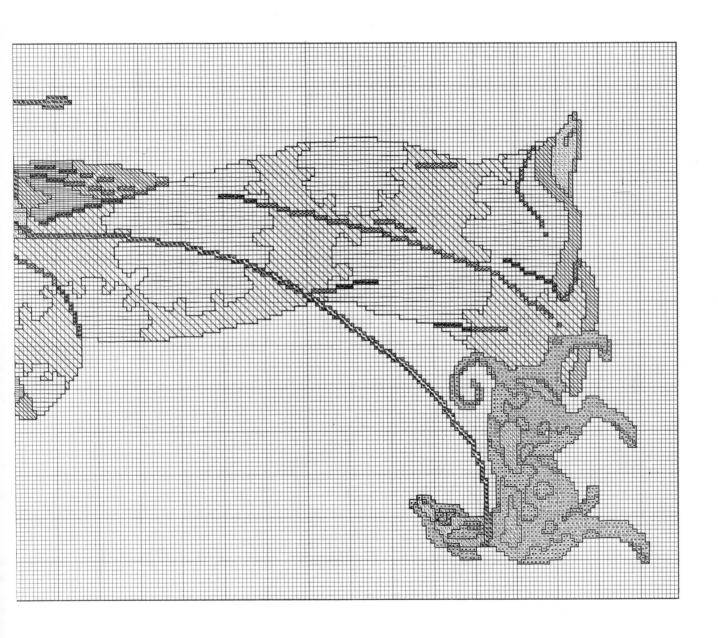

JAPANESE MAN

This figure is also from the famous Hikone Screen. The Hikone Screen was so admired that it was copied more than once, and some of the copies became almost as famous as the original.

The Hikone Screen belongs to one of the most interesting periods in Japanese history and art. What had once been a society of warring feudal lords was turning into a unified country with a class structure that included nobility, landowners, peasants, well-to-do merchants, and an urban middle class, as well as a working class. The middle class were business people and financiers. They sometimes became quite wealthy and had a great deal of money to spend on theater, on geisha houses, on clothing, and on works of art.

The subjects of art, which before this time had been limited to religious themes and nature, now included representations of the daily life of the city. Servants and working people were included in the portrayals of the leisure-time activities of the rich patrons.

When worked on 14-mesh mono canvas, this design will measure 10½ inches by 21½ inches. Cut a piece of canvas 14½ inches by 25½ inches, and bind the edges.

THE PATERNAYAN COLORS ARE:

386   LIGHT BLUE (*lines in robe*)

365   DARK BLUE (*robe*)

453   LIGHT GOLD

445   MEDIUM GOLD (*clothing*)

145   LIGHT BROWN (*lines in clothing*)

020   LIGHT TAN (*shading in flesh*)

005   WHITE (*flesh*)

492   BEIGE

104   BROWN

242   RED (*belt, collar*)

015   YELLOW BEIGE (*background*)

050   BLACK (*hair*)

496   LIGHT BEIGE (*tassels on belt, outline of foot*)

JAPANESE MAN

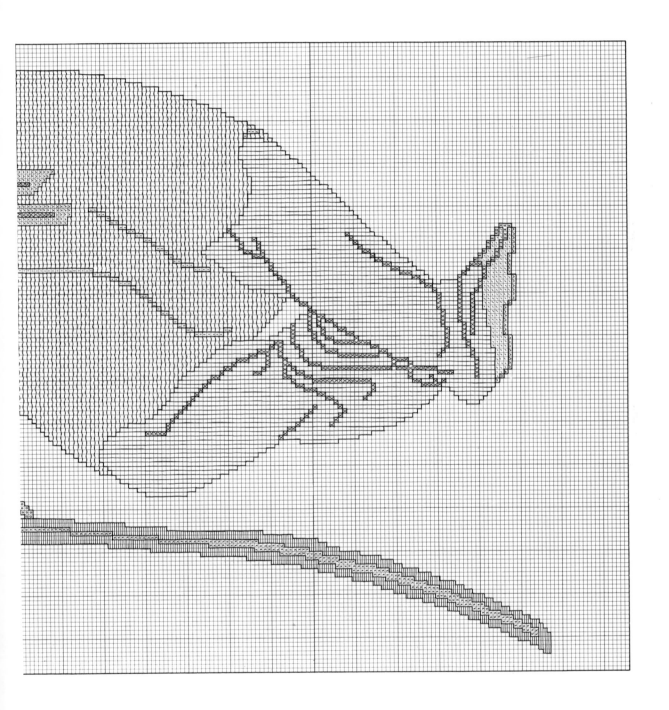

BAT MEDALLION

This design appears at first glance to be simply a composition of abstract, leaflike forms and graceful curves. But if you study it closely, you can see that it is really an abstraction of a bat flying, as Chinese bats are often portrayed, head downward. (Bats were presumed to have very heavy brains!)

This design was adapted from a pattern on a Chinese costume. In this case the word *costume* doesn't mean theatrical dress, but refers to garments or robes worn on special occasions by royalty, nobility, and lesser officials. These special robes were always of silk and were woven and embroidered to indicate the wearer's status. The status could be shown by the sumptuousness of the fabric or by the quality of the needlework ornamentation and the designs. The embroidery often included the rank badge and motifs that stood for happiness, good fortune, wealth, or long life. The bat was a favorite symbol for designs that incorporated such hopes.

When worked on 14-mesh mono canvas, this design will measure 16 by 16 inches. Cut a piece of canvas 20 inches by 20 inches, and bind the edges.

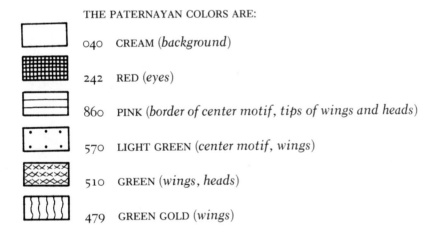

THE PATERNAYAN COLORS ARE:

040   CREAM (*background*)

242   RED (*eyes*)

860   PINK (*border of center motif, tips of wings and heads*)

570   LIGHT GREEN (*center motif, wings*)

510   GREEN (*wings, heads*)

479   GREEN GOLD (*wings*)

BAT MEDALLION

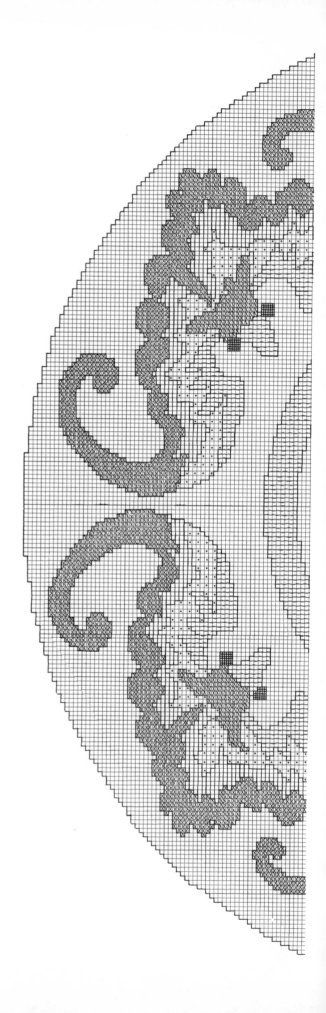

CALLIGRAPHY DESIGN: LONGEVITY

Chinese writing isn't based on an alphabet with each letter representing one sound, as our alphabet is. It has evolved instead from picture language, or pictographs. The characters actually are very simplified pictures or ideographs of things. The oldest known Chinese writings were scratched on bone and tortoiseshell and have been dated as belonging to the Shang dynasty (1523 to 1028 B.C.). But it is evident from that calligraphy that writing was a well-developed art much earlier. Throughout the centuries, these ideographic characters have acquired special meanings, and when put together, although they may look like a single figure to us, they represent an entire sentence or a complicated idea.

Because Chinese writing originated as little pictures, it has a significance to the Chinese and the Japanese much like that of painting. Beautiful writing is often mounted and displayed as if it were a fine work of art. Formerly anyone studying painting in the Orient was required to learn to write well as a first step in communicating through art. Painting and calligraphy were handled as one subject in Chinese instruction books.

This calligraphic design, adapted from a tapestry, stands for longevity. It is decorated with flowers, which the Chinese so adore, and which seem to indicate here that all life is constantly renewed. Spring flowers are yearly evidence of this renewal.

When worked on 14-mesh mono canvas, this design will measure 15 inches by 17½ inches. Cut a piece of canvas 19 inches by 21½ inches, and bind the edges.

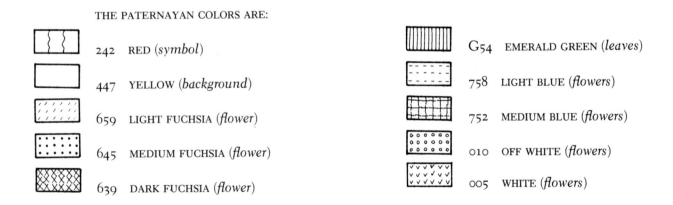

THE PATERNAYAN COLORS ARE:

242   RED (*symbol*)

447   YELLOW (*background*)

659   LIGHT FUCHSIA (*flower*)

645   MEDIUM FUCHSIA (*flower*)

639   DARK FUCHSIA (*flower*)

G54   EMERALD GREEN (*leaves*)

758   LIGHT BLUE (*flowers*)

752   MEDIUM BLUE (*flowers*)

010   OFF WHITE (*flowers*)

005   WHITE (*flowers*)

CALLIGRAPHY

DESIGN:

LONGEVITY

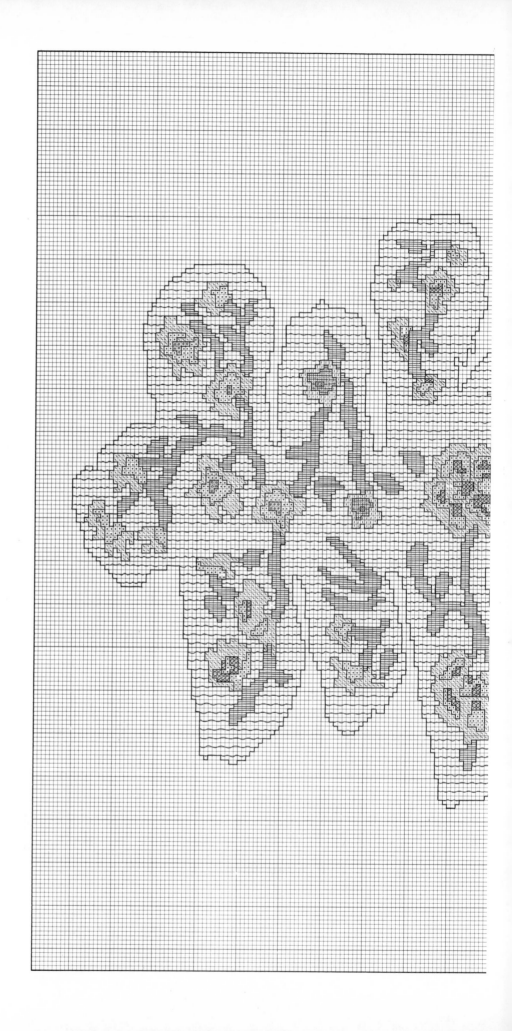

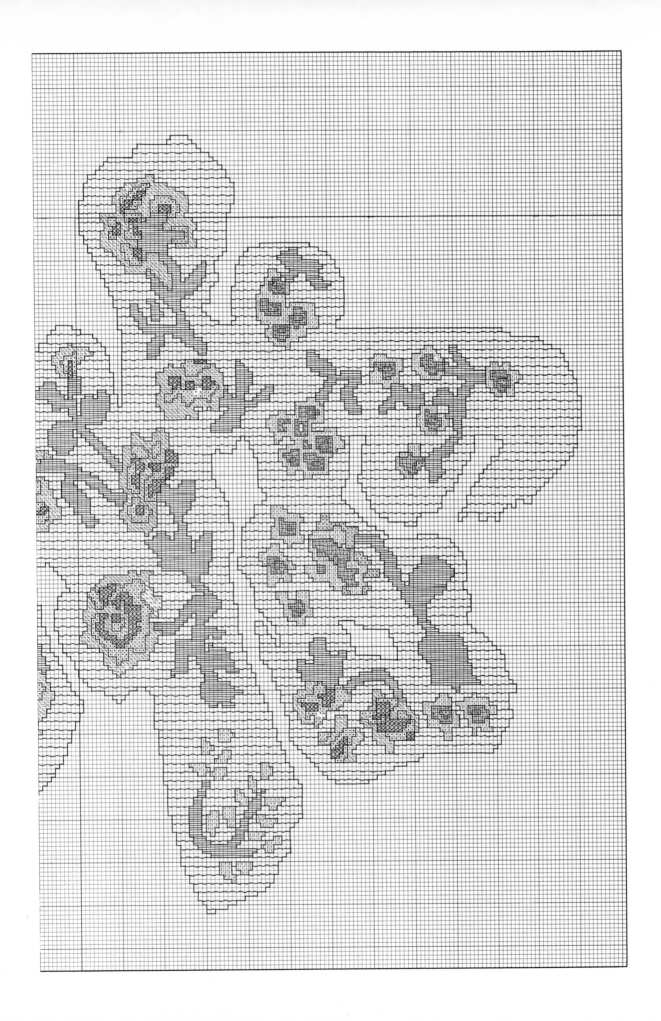

BLUE CRANE

The crane in this design was found nestling in a very lovely antique Chinese dish.

The crane is probably the second most commonly depicted bird in Chinese art after the mythical phoenix, but only one of several species known in China received the honor of being immortalized in legend and symbol. That one is the Manchurian crane, whose coloring distinguishes it from other species. Though it is said to breed in eastern Siberia and northern Manchuria, it spends the winter on the lower Yangtze, so it is well known throughout large areas of China. It is believed to have remarkable powers of longevity.

The crane is quite often painted together with the sun and a fir tree, which are also symbolic of long life.

A Chinese writer by the name of San Ts'ai T'u Hui declared that after a series of various stages of development and change, at the age of one hundred and sixty years, "the male and female gaze at each other, the pupils of their eyes fixed unblinkingly. In this way the female becomes pregnant. After six hundred years they drink but do not eat."

When worked on 14-mesh mono canvas, this design will measure 14 inches by 14 inches. Cut a piece of canvas 18 inches by 18 inches, and bind the edges.

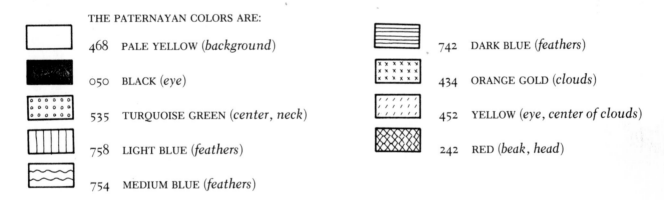

THE PATERNAYAN COLORS ARE:

468 PALE YELLOW (*background*)

050 BLACK (*eye*)

535 TURQUOISE GREEN (*center, neck*)

758 LIGHT BLUE (*feathers*)

754 MEDIUM BLUE (*feathers*)

742 DARK BLUE (*feathers*)

434 ORANGE GOLD (*clouds*)

452 YELLOW (*eye, center of clouds*)

242 RED (*beak, head*)

BLUE CRANE

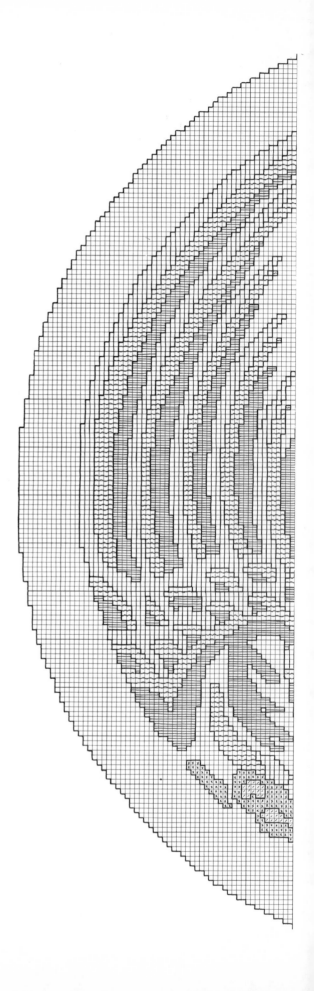

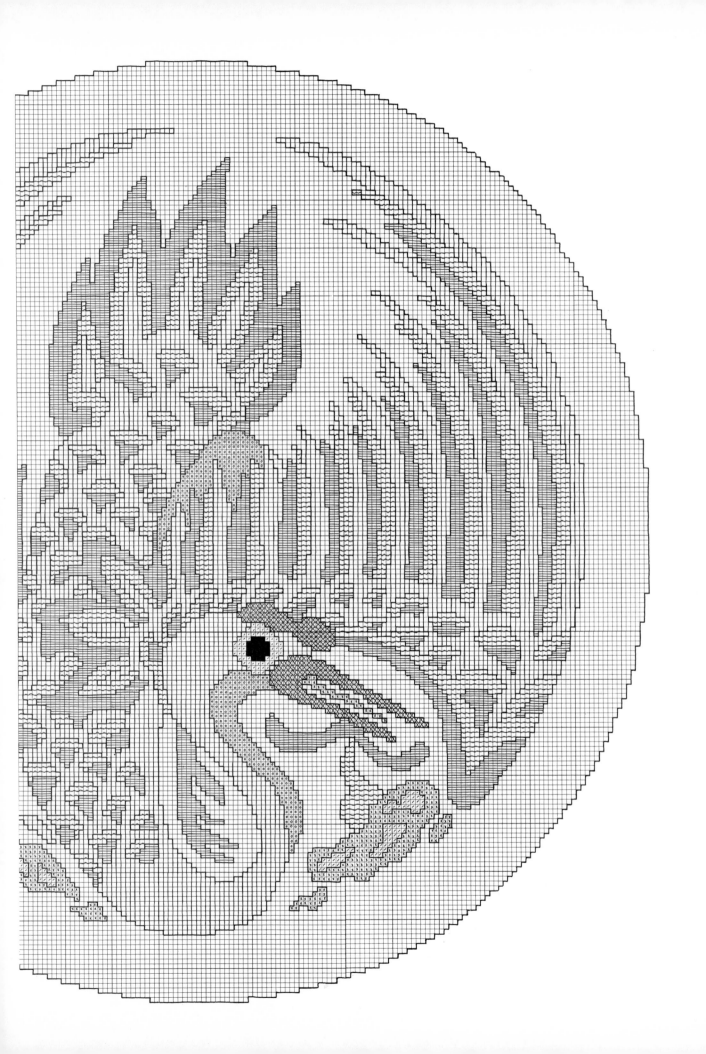

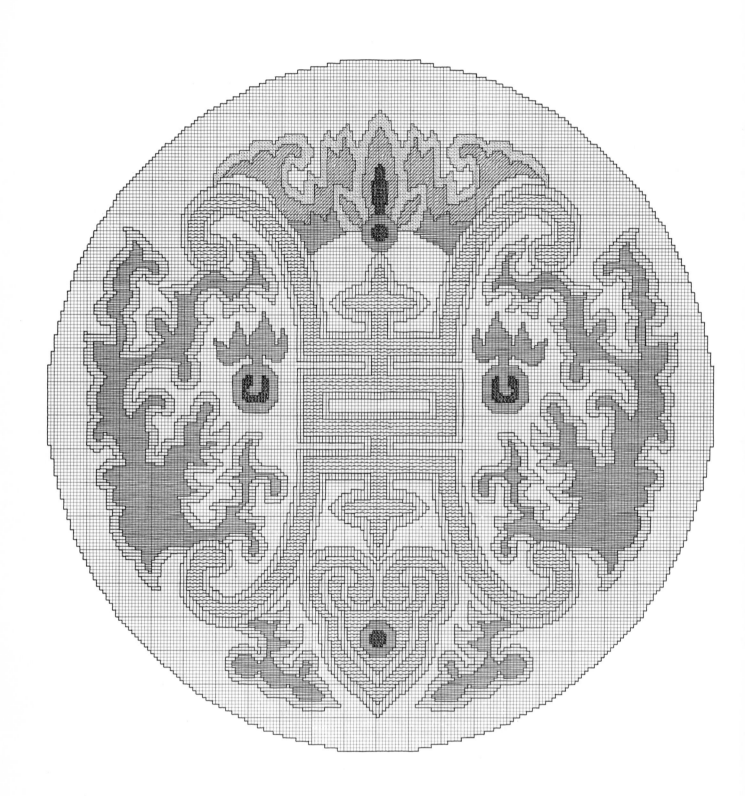

BATS—SYMMETRICAL DESIGN

The stage setting has always been rather simple in China, therefore great emphasis has been put on the theatrical costume. Grand designs of symbolic significance, such as the bat, would be embroidered onto elaborate costumes.

Depending on how the design is interpreted, it loses its realistic form and attains an identity of its own, depending on the artist's imagery. Some are loose irregular designs; some are structured, almost geometric, such as the one interpreted here.

When worked on 14-mesh mono canvas, this design will measure 14 inches by 14 inches. Cut a piece of canvas 18 inches by 18 inches, and bind the edges.

THE PATERNAYAN COLORS ARE:

014 VERY PALE PINK (*background*)

278 LIGHT TERRA COTTA (*design on left and right*)

215 DARK TERRA COTTA (*design on left and right*)

756 LIGHT BLUE (*inner design*)

752 MEDIUM BLUE (*inner design*)

391 LIGHT GRAY (*design at top*)

346 DARK GRAY (*design at top*)

108 CHARCOAL (*design at top*)

BATS—SYMMETRICAL DESIGN

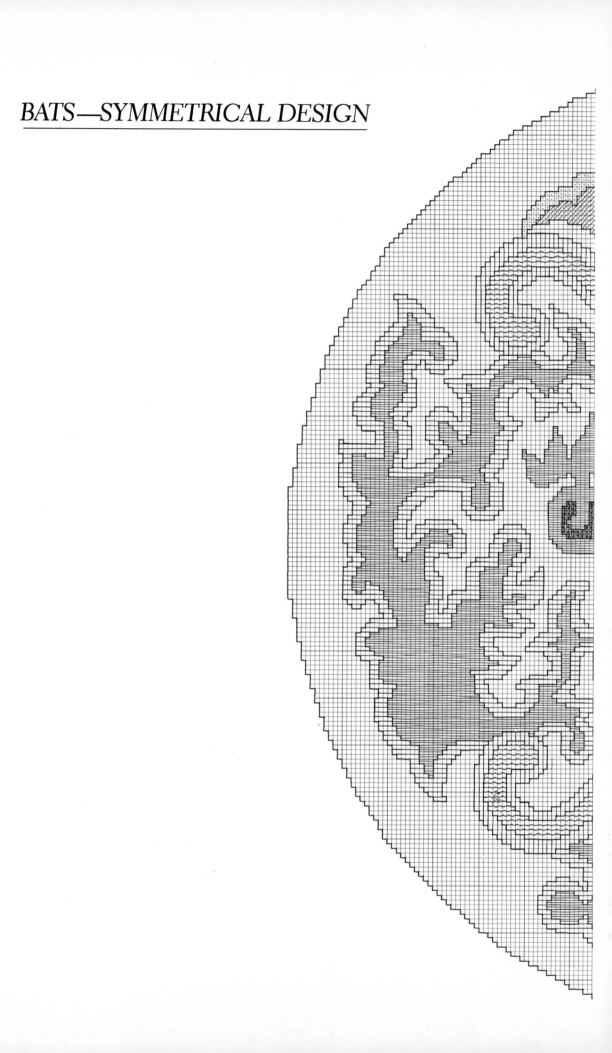

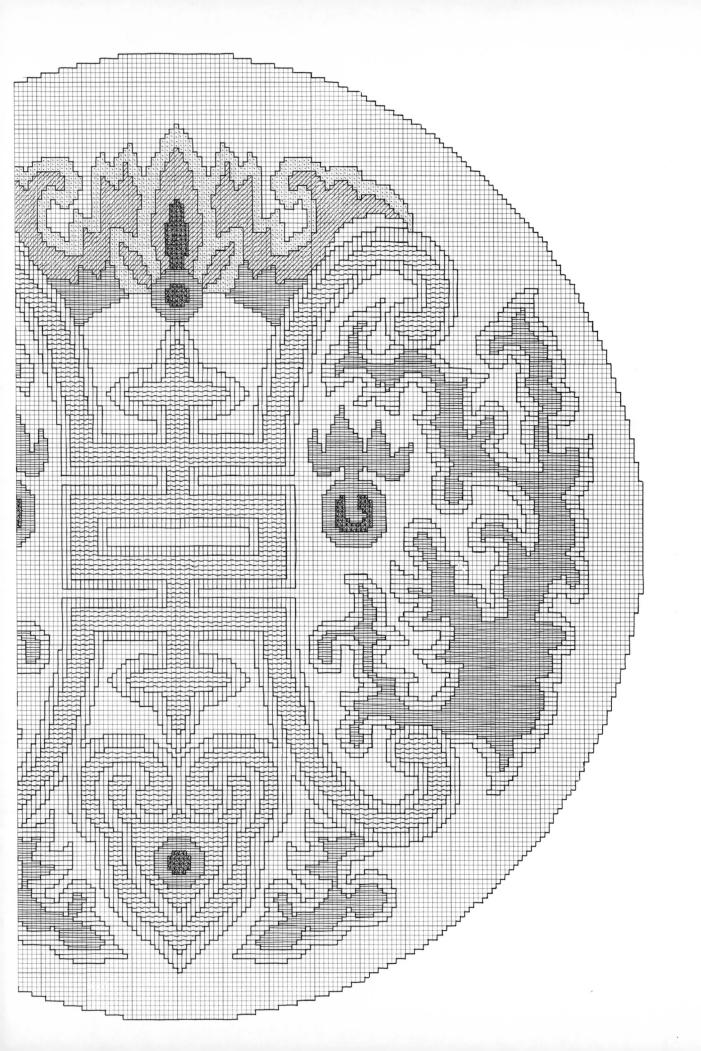

Sources for Supplies

Paternayan Bros.
312 East 95th Street
New York, NY 10028

Persian yarn available through retail distribution.

Empire Wood Carving Co.
1640 Walnut Street
Chicago, Il. 60612

Fire screen available through retail distribution.

BIBLIOGRAPHY

Baker, Muriel. *The ABC's of Canvas Embroidery*. Sturbridge, Mass.: Old Sturbridge Village, 1968.

————. *The XYZ's of Canvas Embroidery*. Sturbridge, Mass.: Old Sturbridge Village, 1968.

Camman, Schuyler. *Embroidery Techniques in Old China*. Archives of the Chinese Art Society in America, XVI, 1962.

Caulfield, Sophia Frances Anne. *The Dictionary of Needlework*. London, England: L. Upcott Gill, 1882.

Clabburn, Pamela. *The Needlework Dictionary*. New York: William Morrow & Co., 1976.

Cox, Hebe. *Canvas Embroidery*. London, England: Mills & Boon, Ltd., 1960.

de Iturralde, Mary Selbey. *Needlepoint: The Sport of Queens*. Williamsburg: Williamsburg Gazette, 1942.

Fisher, Joan. *The Creative Art of Needlepoint Tapestry*. London, England: Hamlyn, 1972.

Gartner, Louis J. *Needlepoint Design*. New York: William Morrow & Co., 1970.

Hanley, Hope. *Needlepoint in America*. New York: Charles Scribner's Sons, 1960.

Jenyns, Soame. *A Background to Chinese Painting*. New York: Shocken Books, 1966.

Jourdain, Margaret, and Jenyns, R. Soame. *Chinese Export Art in the Eighteenth Century*. London, England: Spring Books, Hamlyn House, 1967.

Juliano, Annette L. *Art of the Six Dynasties*. New York: China House Gallery, China Institute in America, 1976.

Mailey, Jean. *Embroidery of Imperial China*. New York: China House Gallery, China Institute in America, 1978.

Mountfield, David. *The Antique Collector's Illustrated Dictionary*. London, England: Hamlyn, 1975.

Munsterberg, Hugo. *Dragons in Chinese Art*. New York: China House Gallery, China Institute in America, 1972.

Noma, Seeroku. *Japanese Costume and Textile Arts*. Trans. by Armins Nikovskis. New York: Weatherhill, 1974.

Picken, Mary Brooks, and White, Doris, with Claire Valentine. *Needlepoint for Everyone*. New York: Harper & Row, 1970.

Pirest, Alan, and Simon, Paule. *Chinese Textiles*. New York: Metropolitan Museum of Art, 1931.

Swan, Susan Burrow. *A Winterthur Guide to American Needlepoint*. New York: Crown Publishers, 1976.

Weissman, Julia, and Hemphill, Herbert. *The Fabric of the State*. New York: Museum of American Folk Art, 1972.

Weldon's Encyclopedia of Needlework. London, England: The Waverly Book Co.

Yun-wu, Wang. *Tapestry in the Collection of the National Palace Museum*. Tokyo, Japan: Gakken Co., Ltd.

ABOUT THE AUTHOR

Eva Brent, one of this country's most talented needlepoint designers, whose work is sold through the best shops, has studied art since the age of twelve. Born in Hungary, she studied at the School of Fine and Applied Art in Budapest, was an art major at Manchester College in Indiana, and completed her education at the Parsons School of Design. After entering the field of advertising as an art director, she lacked artistic freedom and has therefore chosen to become an artist in her own right.